praise for **Loosen Their Lips**

True masters don't need to promote themselves—they lead with humility, wisdom, and grace. Ellen Naylor is one of those rare few. I'm incredibly fortunate to call her a friend and mentor. Her book is a timely reminder —especially in our post-COVID world—of the lost art of real human connection and the power of genuine conversation. Elicitation isn't just a skill; it's a practice we need to revive, and Ellen shows us how.

—Jay Nakagawa
Former Chairman, SCIP
(Strategic Consortium of Intelligence Professionals)

It is a true privilege to review Ellen Naylor's second book, **Loosen Their Lips.** *With over three decades in the Competitive Intelligence (CI) field, I consider this work a masterclass in the art and science of communication and elicitation.*

While acknowledging the growing role of technological tools—such as generative AI—for enhancing efficiency, Naylor astutely reminds us that nothing can replace the power of genuine human-to-human interaction. She underscores the importance of thoughtful preparation and, more critically, developing a deep understanding of the individual you're engaging with.

The book is rich with insights from industry experts, and Naylor's research and real-world case studies compellingly illustrate the enduring value of the "human factor" in successful elicitation.

Whether you're new to Competitive Intelligence or a seasoned professional, **Loosen Their Lips** *offers practical wisdom and strategic guidance that will elevate your skills and mindset.*

—Laurie Young
Former Vice Chairman, SCIP

Ellen Naylor's latest masterpiece, **Loosen their Lips,** *is a natural successor to John Nolan's Confidential. Its conversational and instructive style brings teaching points to life through Naylor's project experience and insights and third-party comments. Key concepts include Nolan's Elicitation Conversational Hourglass, Elicitation Simplified, the 5Ps, and DiSC. Each chapter ends with a summary and actionable challenges, making this book invaluable for those seeking to understand human interactions better and for curious minds desiring richer, more human contact in our screen-based world.*

—Andrew Beurschgens
Market and Customer Insight Leader

Some of the simplest concepts … like listening with intent … can and often do offer the most powerful insights. These are lessons you've learned because you are always paying attention and in the moment. **Loosen Their Lips** *is full of these nuggets of wisdom and will be of value to anyone who seeks deep human insights for gaining advantages. And who won't benefit from that?*

—Dr. Craig S. Fleisher
Professor, 17x Author

Loosen their Lips

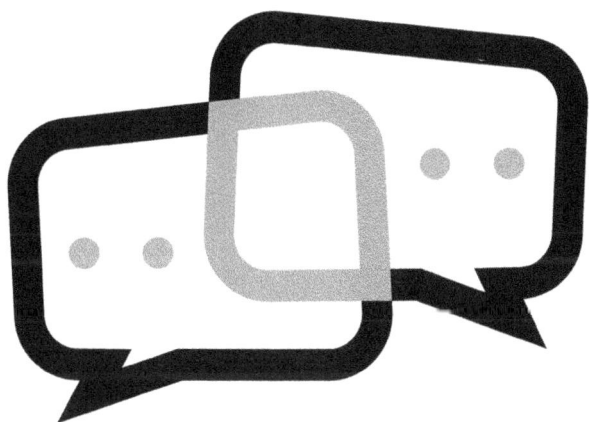

How to Capture the Information You Seek During a Conversation

Ellen Naylor

Author of **Win/Loss Analysis**

Books in bulk can be ordered from the publisher or author:
Ellen@EllenNaylor.com or +1 720-480-9499 (phone or text)

Cover and Interior Design: Rebecca Finkel, F + P Graphic Design
Editors: Rodgers Naylor and Judith Briles
Book Consultant: Judith Briles, The Book Shepherd

ISBN paperback: 978-0-9972722-3-9
ISBN eBook: 978-0-9972722-4-6
ISBN Audiobook: 978-0-9972722-5-3

Business | Communication | Competitive Intelligence

Printed in United States of America

This book is dedicated to
John Nolan whose elicitation expertise
and knowledge sharing inspired me
to write *Loosen Their Lips*.

Also By

Win/Loss Analysis:
How to Capture and Keep the Business You Want

Contents

Author's Note vii

CHAPTER 1 Why Real Conversations Matter 1

PART ONE Interview-Conversation Process 7

CHAPTER 2 Description: Interview-Conversation Process 9

CHAPTER 3 Plan: Establish Goals 19

CHAPTER 4 Plan: Research: Warm Up the Interview
The Collection Continuum 27

CHAPTER 5 Plan: Research: The Collection Continuum:
Digital Sources 33

CHAPTER 6 Plan: Research: The Collection Continuum:
Human Sources 41

CHAPTER 7 Plan: Prepare Your Introduction and Ethics 51

CHAPTER 8 Pre-Execution: Get Grounded 59

CHAPTER 9 Pre-Execution: Set Your Intention 69

CHAPTER 10 Pre-Execution: Motivation............................. 81

CHAPTER 11 Pre-Execution: Communication Style:
D.i.S.C and EQ 89

CHAPTER 12 Pre-Execution: Unique: Who is She or He?......... 97

CHAPTER 13 Execute: Execute the Call 103

CHAPTER 14 Execute: Build Rapport............................... 109

CHAPTER 15 Execute: Observe Verbal and Nonverbal
Communication for Cues............................ 117

CHAPTER 16 Execute: Be Flexible 131

CHAPTER 17 Execute: Listen to the Response 141

CHAPTER 18 Execute: Deception, Misinformation, Omission .. 149

CHAPTER 19 Execute: Be Visually Friendly 157

CHAPTER 20 Execute: Probe the Response 163

CHAPTER 21 Analyze: Analyze the Call 169

PART TWO Elicitation 175

CHAPTER 22 Elicitation Introduction 177

CHAPTER 23 Elicitation: The Process 185

CHAPTER 24 John Nolan's Elicitation
Conversational Hourglass 191

CHAPTER 25 Elicitation Techniques: Case Studies 197

CHAPTER 26 Friendly Elicitation Techniques 203

CHAPTER 27 Provocative Elicitation Techniques 213

CHAPTER 28 Two Important Elicitation Techniques 225

CHAPTER 29 Combining Elicitation Techniques and
Bonus Elicitation Techniques! 231

CHAPTER 30 Elicitation Simplified 237

CHAPTER 31 My Final Thoughts 239

Endnotes 245

Ellen Naylor 248

How to Work with Ellen Naylor 250

In Gratitude 252

Author's Note

I feel that society is reducing the importance, need,
or desire to have a conversation with another human being.

Years ago, a company hired me to start its competitive intelligence program. My first step was to interview a recently hired executive to gauge his need for and perception of competitive intelligence.

I had prepped the newly minted competitive intelligence (CI) team on conducting such a conversation, so they would feel comfortable taking a lead in this conversation as they would meet the executive at the client's US company headquarters. Meanwhile, I sat in my Colorado office to quietly observe and mentor the team. We had researched the executive's background. He'd been at a large corporation in the Asia-Pacific. Neither my CI team nor their contacts had met him yet. So, none of us knew how he'd be motivated or what his needs for competitive intelligence would be, or if he even knew what it was.

Early in the conversation he said, "I am not really sure if we need an internal competitive intelligence program."

No one, including me, had expected that he would question the need for a competitive intelligence program. After all, that's what I had been hired to help develop! There was a long silence from the CI team, so I broke the silence by asking, "What makes you think this?"

This simple question opened him up. We listened to him for 20 minutes as he told us about his work history. What was most important to learn was his bias as a former executive at McKinsey, where he had ready access to information on competitors from their extensive library and connections. I credited the company and suggested that McKinsey would be a great resource for one-off projects, but that he would benefit by using internal company employees to develop an ongoing competitive intelligence process. Plus, it would be more economical as there would be no additional cost. This would be part of their jobs.

As it turned out, this executive had the best understanding of competitive intelligence of any of his peers at the company. But it was my simple question that opened him up to an informative conversation. He listened. We listened. And he was on board to develop an internal competitive intelligence program. As I loosened his lips and opened my ears, we developed a relationship and made the sale.

With each rung of digital technical evolution—the Internet, social media, and AI in its many forms—it's become clear to me that society is reducing the importance, need, or desire to have a conversation with another human being. Many of you have become addicted to your screens, especially your smartphones. Taking all this time to be social media-connected has reduced your time and capacity for solitude that nurtures reflection, creativity and critical thinking. And for most people, it is necessary to have some downtime.

Solitude helps you prepare and reach out for conversations. You are in danger of losing the perspective that can only be gained by talking to another person.

Sherry Turkle expresses it so well in *Reclaiming Conversation: The Power of Talk in a Digital Age.*

We are tempted to think that our little sips of online connection add up to a big gulp of real conversation. But they don't.

When you interact with someone online, you feel and sense the person you're communicating with less.

Email, texting and social media all have their place … but no matter how valuable, they do not substitute for conversation.

In a conversation, you are called upon to see things from another's point of view. You live in a technical world and are always in communication. And yet you are sacrificing conversation for mere digital connection.

The more people interact online, the less they seem to truly hear one another. Miscommunication and noncommunication flourish. When you interact with someone online, you feel and sense the person you're communicating with less. Likes and hearts don't carry the same emotional force as conversation and eye-to-eye contact. The Internet ignores or undermines human conditions such as empathy, deep relationships, sustained conversation, compromise, compassion and other emotions like fear and anger.

Business conversation is the focus of this book. Conversation is a human need and is the best way to build and keep relationships. It is also an effective way to build trust if you're willing to listen to the other person with an open mind, one that is willing to change. It's also the best way to learn information that isn't on the Internet.

And it is WHY this book was written by me and edited by humans without the assistance of artificial intelligence!

Ellen

chapter one

Why Real Conversations Matter

Follow my approach to
planning and having a conversation.

The information I gained in the stories that I share throughout *Loosen Their Lips* was only possible through conversation with another person—often several! The information collected and insights were used to make smart, informed decisions.

You don't get this depth of information and insights from the Internet, social media, or anywhere other than from fellow human beings. You also develop a relationship with these people, where you can reach out to them in the future and get deep information and make a difference in their lives and yours. Yet, too many are fearful of having conversations these days.

Why is that? My years of using live conversations have led me to believe that most feel that "they can't get it right" the first time they say or think it. They can't edit a live conversation like they can with text, social media or email. But many forget there can be a dark side to not having live, in-person conversations. It is not uncommon for the receiver of digital messages to misinterpret them. They lack the emotions and feelings conveyed from voice and nonverbal expressions during a conversation.

Loosen Their Lips encapsulates my 40-plus years of experience learning how to find what you're looking for most expeditiously and ethically during a conversation. My clients refer to it as my superpower. I have never failed to find out what they are looking for by talking to others, whether on a cold call or a scheduled conversation. People just seem to share what they know with me. This happens socially as well. I hear the story of their lives seemingly without asking.

I intend to help you learn how to find the information you're looking for during a conversation. You have limited time to accomplish this, so you will learn how to guide the conversation. Follow my approach to planning and having a conversation. You will be more efficient during your conversations because you have prepared in the many ways that I share in this book!

You also need to be in the right frame of mind to do conversational research. Preparing your initial greeting and questions are just the beginning.

How do you psych yourself up to have these conversations? You will get my superpower tips starting with Chapter 2. My success rate went up 150% when I:

1. Learned how I come across in a conversation, and people's impressions of me.

2. Quickly assessed how the person I conversed with liked to be communicated with.

3. Factored in the other person's sharing disposition.

4. Learned how to get in the zone to be focused on the other person before our conversation.

5. Made a specific intention as to how the person would feel at the end of our conversation.

I would be remiss if I didn't include an interviewer's super-power, elicitation techniques—another game-changer! I was using them unknowingly for years, but the superpower is using them consciously … and loosening lips!

Many of the stories I'll be sharing come from my world: the world of competitive intelligence (CI).

Competitive intelligence is a field that is driven by human relationships.

When I tell people I work in competitive intelligence, I often get a deer-in-the-headlights look. Or I'll get, "I know what you do. You're a spy." Many also associate it with corporate espionage or dumpster diving. It is not! However, due to the confidential nature of competitive intelligence, I have not disclosed any company names in this book.

There are as many definitions of CI as there are people who do it. It is not a discipline that neatly fits into an elevator pitch. Here's my definition and how it functions in organizations.

Competitive intelligence is a continuous activity that provides an ongoing update of activities in the marketplace. A functioning CI process will provide signals or early warning that allow a company to act first in anticipation of a competitor's moves or to adopt or counteract new technologies that will impact its industry.

Competitive intelligence helps companies better understand their competitive environment to make sound business decisions, and to uncover opportunities and threats. CI includes all the factors that impact a company's ability to compete: suppliers, customers, distributors, competitors and potential competitors.

CI is unique in that it's a people-centric activity that draws on personnel from different areas of the company to cooperate in gathering and sharing competitive and market developments. It's also heavily reliant on technology to monitor the competitive environment and increasingly to analyze it.

Keep in mind that competitive intelligence is valued differently by your clients. Executives value foresight, strategic CI that gives them insight into the marketplace, rivals and exciting opportunities. Sales values CI to provide what they need to win more deals. Product managers value CI to knowingly develop superior products.

The reality is that you use competitive intelligence to make important decisions such as:

- Which house to buy in which neighborhood.
- What company you want to work for.

Also more routinely:

- Preparing for job interviews.
- Shopping deals for vacation destinations.
- Observing potential versus buying customers at my husband's art festivals.

I like Zena Applebaum's description of skills to do CI from *A Practical Guide to Competitive Intelligence.*

> Competitive intelligence (CI) is not market research, it is not strategy, and it is not sales enablement. But it is also **all** of those things. There are many hard skills in CI that you need to know: how to gather and analyze data; how to elicit human intelligence (HUMINT); and how to run reports and think big. But CI is also about softer skills, the set of

competencies that includes but is not limited to curiosity, research ability, relationship building, synthesis, communication, and flexibility.

Victoria Richard Hanna, another author of *A Practical Guide to Competitive Intelligence,* adds, "You also need people who will challenge you and your assumptions and help you be as inclusive in your work as possible."

It is wise to have those around you who will challenge you. It is an effective way to become aware of and to combat your blind spots and biases. It's a battle we all fight as humans. You are who you are, a product of your upbringing, health, race, gender, age, economic status, culture and life experiences. Other people, especially those who challenge you, give you a different perspective, often expanding it. You need to be open to that.

Competitive intelligence is a field that is driven by human relationships. For your clients and prospects if you can't connect with fellow employees, influencers outside of their company and customers, you are ineffective.

Loosen Their Lips focuses on the human side of competitive intelligence, which is getting the person you're talking with to share the knowledge or insight that you're looking for. The processes and techniques that I share in any conversation aren't inclusive to just your work. They are effective with your kids too! I even used these skills to find our cats, Freddie and Carlos.

Doing this for over four decades, I know my techniques work with my friends and neighbors. But this book focuses on professional business conversations. Conversation is not perfect. It comes out of your lips, and yes, you are vulnerable and will make mistakes. Just do it! You're human and so are they!

Part One details the sequence of a business conversation all the way from planning it, conducting it, and analyzing if you reached your goal, what you learned, and what gaps might remain. It's the foundation. Without it solidly in place, Part Two won't stick.

Part Two builds on the same sequence as the business conversation detailed in Part One. Additionally, it includes the specific strategies and tactics of using elicitation techniques to gain even more information during your business conversation! Don't skip to Part Two ... but make sure to read Part One first. It solidifies your foundation, along with all the building blocks and process to hold a conversation. You will want to follow and understand those building blocks to have an effective business conversation before adding elicitation techniques to your skill set.

If you desire to learn how to be an ethical, efficient, and effective conversationalist who captures the information you seek every time, let's begin. I'm honored to be your guide.

In today's fast-paced, overly automated, and digitally driven society, humanity is becoming the new premium.
—**Celinne Da Costa,** author of *If Hearts Could Talk*

Interview-Conversation Process

Conversation is the cornerstone
of humanity. The human presence,
sensitivity and voice are irreplaceable.

—Ellen Naylor

chapter two

Description: Interview-Conversation Process

In today's era of disinformation,
misinformation, fake news, and fake videos,
it's even more important to have live conversations.

Conversation represents one of the aspects of "art" in competitive intelligence. Intuition plays a key role in conversation as there are no models to follow. You need to be very alert to the other person to keep him engaged, often by letting him talk about himself, which makes him feel heard and important.

I have been working in competitive intelligence since 1985. *Win/Loss Analysis: How to Capture and Keep the Business You Want* was published in 2016. I have been influenced by many experts for this book, including those who shared their stories. My key influencer was John Nolan, the author of *Confidential: Uncover Your Competitors' Top Business Secrets Legally and Quickly —and Protect Your Own*, published in 1999. Human nature and motivation have changed very little since then. In an interview in the *Competitive Intelligence Magazine* in 2014, Nolan said, "The best collector is a connector." And he wasn't talking about social media followers!

Much has changed since he published his work in 1999. The digital world has exploded. John Nolan said he would imagine what the person on the other end of the telephone line looked like and then settle into a great conversation. These days there is no need for a cold call with all the digital information out there. Thanks to the Internet, videos, podcasts, and social media, you can see and listen to just about anyone before your conversation with her. Of course, the same is true of you … *you are also visible* on the Internet and social media.

Most people find telephone calls an annoyance unless they're scheduled—and maybe even then. Thank you, robocalling. Most of your conversations probably take place on video calls. So, your powers of observation go far beyond the voice and words during these conversations.

I was coaching a client and several people were in attendance, including the client's boss. He was skeptical about the value of doing Win/Loss interviews and analysis, the topic of our discussion. I was saying that a person's body position of arms crossed in front and leaning back indicates a lack of interest or openness. About 20 minutes into our session, I reminded them that I had a full view of them seated in their conference room. His boss was in both positions and immediately changed his body position … too late. He had already revealed himself.

Like John Nolan, the focus of my conversations is to acquire the information and/or the intelligence I or my clients need to make informed decisions. When I take on a project, I assume that most companies have access to similar information from the Internet, including videos, social media and AI. We have so many choices of ways to consume information. In today's era of disinformation, misinformation, fake news, and fake videos, it's even more important to have live conversations.

Companies with strong people networks have a competitive advantage. Yet, many don't want to invest their time with humans, deferring to what's found online while sitting or standing at their computers or using smartphones. Now with generative AI and who knows what's next, I fear people will rely too much on a digital brain to

Intuition plays a key role in conversation as there are no models to follow.

do their thinking for them, reducing their creativity. On the other hand, I use AI to learn more about those I'll be speaking with, to find them, and to formulate questions I might ask.

Conversation and Competitive Intelligence

You get answers during conversations with sources you think know the information you're looking for to make important decisions. Often, you are told things you don't even know to ask about, which can be so valuable. Sources include fellow employees, customers, industry experts, competitors, suppliers, among others. More than 80% of what you wish you knew resides in the minds of fellow employees.

Competitive intelligence is not just about the competition! One of my clients had a problem, and his problem, and resolution, was an ideal example of how competitive intelligence works.

His company was hauling tons of powder, a byproduct of their manufacturing process, to the dump. This was a major expense. He didn't like the environmental impact of trashing this volume of powder. His question to me was: Is there a way to generate revenue by selling the byproduct powder? He was unsure if there was a value to such a product.

Together we looked at the market and hypothesized that the concrete industry would be a good target. The byproduct powder could be added to the cement mixture to make it more durable. The addition of this powder would prevent the cement from contracting and expanding as much in hot and wintry weather conditions. Think about the weather in Minnesota and Wisconsin or other parts of the world where it gets up to 100° Fahrenheit (38° Celsius) in the summer and commonly down to −20° Fahrenheit (-29° Celsius) in the winter.

I did some digital research and looked at competing products. Then I spoke with prospective companies to learn what they would value from such a powder in cement production. First, I learned that there was plenty of competition, and it seemed like this was not a profitable business. I really lucked out when I happened upon an expert in this space who worked for the US government. He knew all the players and had worked in this market for over 20 years. He told me that no one was making much money in this business.

Competitive intelligence is not just about the competition.

Another factor that hurt my client was the color of their powder, something I hadn't even thought about. It was a dark gray color, and the cement manufacturers preferred a light color closer to white. Some competitors' powders were as durable as my client's but were almost white. They were already shipping it to cement producers. The government expert I interviewed suggested that my client should hold off getting into this market. He believed that there wouldn't be enough demand for their powder and that sadly they should continue hauling it to the dump. So that's what they did.

Two years later, this client contacted me for updated CI. I figured I would get my answer primarily from speaking to the same government expert. But alas, he had retired. Not one to give up easily, I suspected he was still working in the same industry. Happily, I found out that he had formed a consultancy and had a website with contact information. We had a conversation. He told me that the market for this powder was even worse than it had been previously. And he revealed that a couple of the providers had exited this business. Ever the skeptic, I also called the competitors who were anxious to ship me samples. These were not happy conversations.

I felt I had no choice but to report that the market was even worse for my client's byproduct powder than it had been previously.

As often happens, some companies want to push something forward—even if it's a bad idea. My client's management was negotiating 10-year contracts to supply this powder to large cement producers.

I gave them the intelligence they needed to make the right decision. To give them credit, they halted their negotiations. Sadly, it was most cost-effective to keep hauling their byproduct powder to the landfill. They listened and were open to my informed recommendation. The outcome? They thanked me, saying I saved them millions of dollars since that is what it would have cost them to pull out of the long-term contracts with cement producers that they were on the cusp of signing.

Empathy

I worry that people are losing empathy. I love Brené Brown's definition from *Atlas of the Heart*, one of my favorite books:

Empathy, the most powerful tool of compassion, is an emotional skill set that allows us to understand what someone is experiencing and to reflect back that understanding.

Ronda Dearing, Senior Research Director at the Brené Brown Education and Research Group, adds,

Empathy is an other-focused emotion. It draws our attention outward, toward the other person's experience. We only have thoughts of self in order to draw on how our experience can help us understand what the other person is going through.

Daniel Goleman, the pioneering author of *Emotional Intelligence,* adds two factors to empathy:

- Use language the other person understands.
- Care about people.

You can't trust someone who gets you but doesn't care about you.

In the quest to get information from other people during a conversation, you can be self-centered, intense and manipulative. This is bad behavior and can make others feel used by the end of the conversation, or later when they reflect on their conversation with you. That is why I like to be empathetic during any conversation. People don't feel used when they see you care.

You want to gain trust quickly during a conversation. Listening and believing what somebody tells you creates trust and connection.

I will add another factor: Be curious and let the other person know you're curious by asking good questions or making comments that let him know you're listening and want to learn more.

As competitive intelligence professional Kent Potter reminds us, "Interviewing is about driving relationships, not about taking."

OK, enough of a preamble, let's get to the meat of this book: planning and executing conversations ethically, effectively, efficiently and with empathy.

I have noticed three shortcomings in conversation and have been guilty of them on occasion myself!

• Lack of preparation

• Poor listening

• Little contingency planning. Conversations often don't go the way you think they will. You need to be prepared for that!

Interview-Conversation

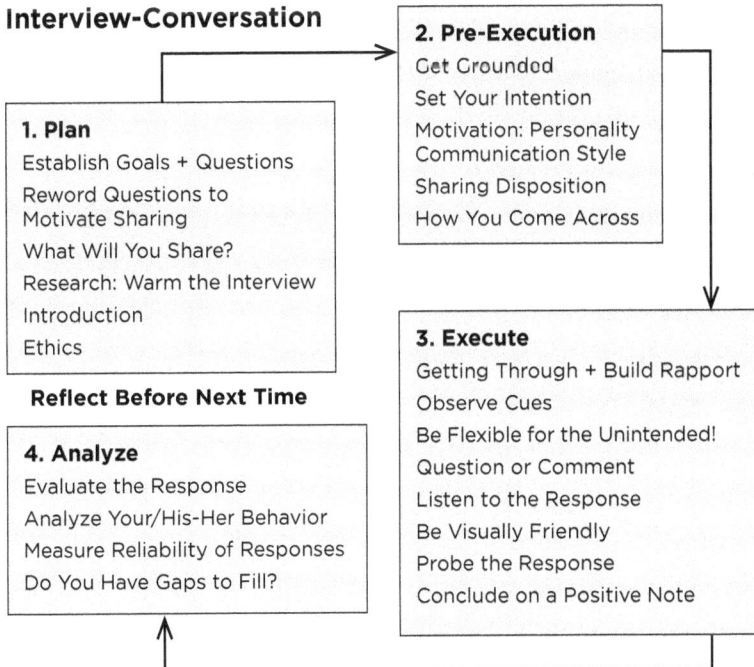

1. Plan
Establish Goals + Questions
Reword Questions to Motivate Sharing
What Will You Share?
Research: Warm the Interview
Introduction
Ethics

2. Pre-Execution
Get Grounded
Set Your Intention
Motivation: Personality
Communication Style
Sharing Disposition
How You Come Across

3. Execute
Getting Through + Build Rapport
Observe Cues
Be Flexible for the Unintended!
Question or Comment
Listen to the Response
Be Visually Friendly
Probe the Response
Conclude on a Positive Note

Reflect Before Next Time

4. Analyze
Evaluate the Response
Analyze Your/His-Her Behavior
Measure Reliability of Responses
Do You Have Gaps to Fill?

©Ellen Naylor, Business Intelligence Source

For an important conversation, I have provided four steps that are broken into multiple chapters under Part One. (Refer to Contents for clarity.)

1. Plan

2. Pre-Execution

3. Execute

4. Analyze

Note that there are **five** planning steps before you have your conversation. There is no need to make a cold call these days with all the information you can find out about a person before you have a conversation. Even if she isn't on social media, which is rare, you can collect information about her profession and industry to warm up the call. Your first goal during a conversation is to quickly get her comfortable talking with you.

You want to be organized! What will you hit her with as soon as she answers the call or appears on the screen? Will this vary? Why? Maybe her expression or tone tells you that she might be more friendly or not.

First impressions are important, and you only get one chance. People make their impressions in **one-tenth** of a second when they see a stranger's face. If you're on an audio call, you get SEVEN seconds to make the right impression through your voice, breathing and the energy that you radiate.

Even if I have worked in the same industry, I take a crash course to learn the business, industry jargon and the person's profession. I'll ask for industry reports from my clients, which they are happy to provide. While I am not the expert that the person

I'm talking to is, I want to understand his space well enough to engage him in a conversation.

**If knowledge is power,
then knowing what we don't know is wisdom.**

—**Adam Grant,** Organizational Psychologist and Professor

chapter three

Plan:
Establish Goals

What do you want to accomplish
during this conversation?

You probably didn't want to read that one of the keys to being
a good conversationalist is to take enough time to prepare. It can
be boring, but if you shortchange this, it shows. You won't get the
same level of engagement. You'll notice that professional TV and
radio interviewers often have a script they refer to on their show.
There is plenty of thought and effort that goes into the preparation
for their talk shows to make them timely and interesting for the
audience. Examples of superstars include:

- Oprah Winfrey, Media Mogul, Philanthropist
- Zanny Minton Beddoes, Editor-in-Chief of *The Economist*
- Terry Gross, Host and Producer of *Fresh Air*

It's also amazing to watch these skilled interviewers direct,
redirect, and even cut off their guest while remaining pleasant
and professional!

Establish Your Goals/Questions

Be clear about what you want to accomplish during this conversation. Usually you have a set time, so be realistic about how much you can cover. I've been guilty of trying to accomplish too much during a 30-minute conversation.

What are the specific objectives of this conversation? Most often, it's three or four major items.

When I refer to a Win/Loss conversation for a client—a call with the customer after a sale is won or lost, I want to learn:

1. The major reasons we won or lost the business.

2. Who else they considered and why.

3. How they made their buying decision.

What questions do you want answered?
Next, you develop the questions you want to ask to achieve your objectives. Under the objective, "How they made their buying decision," you want to know:

- Who participated in decision-making?

- Did they have a team?

- Did they use a grid for decision-making to assess the competitors?

- Is that something they are willing to share?

- Who was the key decision-maker(s)?

- Who were the key influencers?

- What was the role of the procurement department?

- How well did our company's people interact with theirs?

I then make a list of questions to make sure we're covering all the issues my client wants to learn about.

What is a good leading question to get the person talking?
I often start a Win/Loss call by asking the person what he does at the company. Most people like to talk about themselves, and this usually makes them comfortable with me.

What do you need to research first to get informed?
Before each Win/Loss call, I look up the person on the Internet and social media. This usually gives me enough information about what he does at the company and prior work history. We may even have something in common, such as places we've lived, schools we've attended, etc. For other projects, I may need to do a lot more research. There's more detail in the next chapter. *Plan: Research: Warm up the Interview – The Collection Continuum.*

Is there someone you can talk to who might help?
I like to talk with the Account Executive or the Technical Expert for the sale before I reach out to his customer for a Win/Loss call. Salespeople are informative about what happened during the sale, although they have the bias of a seller. They get extra marks if they inform their customer that I'll be reaching out to have a conversation with him.

Reword Questions to Motivate
Now it's time to reorder the questions and think about the right words to use, words that will resonate with the person you will talk to. I will often read the re-ordered/reworded questions out loud to hear how they sound and flow. I'm trying to put myself in the other person's shoes to the extent that I can.

All too often companies are stuck in their own world and forget when talking to a customer to use the customer's language. You're looking for your customer's perspective, not your company's. You want to ask questions that are clearly stated and just ask one question at a time. I start with questions that I think are the easiest for the other person to answer.

I like to anticipate how the other person might answer each question. Like a decision tree, this helps me be prepared for the unexpected since that's often how a conversation goes. A decision tree helps you think where and how to probe more deeply depending on how he answers each question. It can prompt you to think about what questions he might ask you. After all, it's a two-way conversation.

To illustrate the different types of questions, I will use an example from a project. We were hired to gather market intelligence on meters that test and measure electricity. We interviewed about 50 users in the industrial, commercial and handyman worlds. None of these people were on the Internet, so we spent considerable time studying the industry, picking up the industry jargon, and putting together some small talk. Below are some of the questions we used and some of the results.

We started with some **Broad Questions:**

- What do you do at Company X?

- How has this changed in the last few years?

This would get the conversation flowing since people like to talk about themselves. We wanted to know how the market was changing because we sensed that the meters were being used less often than previously. And we wanted to understand why that was. This second question was flattering as we presumed they were market experts without stating it explicitly.

Hypothetical Question: "Which meter do you use? If you bought one again, what brand would you buy?" I thought he might say, "I don't know when I'll buy one again," or something equally vague. Then I wanted to insist, "But if you bought one again, which brand would it be? Make an educated guess." I thought this would be a great way to get some information about the competition—and it was.

Indirect Questions: This example is from Win/Loss interviews for complex software since decision-making is a simple process when buying an electrical measurement meter. I would be talking to an IT professional for this Win/Loss interview.

> "Might you be a key influencer at your company?"
>
> I figured this would get him to tell me something like, "Yes, I presented the business case to the management team."
>
> Then I would say, "So, I suppose the CTO was the key decision-maker?"
>
> And he might say, "No, actually it was our CEO, but the CTO was on the decision-making team."

With this indirect approach, he'll often share more about the decision-making team and the process.

Narrow Questions: Back to the electrical measurement meter conversation.

"Do you install, troubleshoot, repair or maintain equipment? What electrical parameters do you measure at work?" (current, voltage, ohms, etc.) Our client was looking to learn their customer's maximum voltage and amperage requirements for testing. They thought these answers would help them with product development. The tradesmen were happy to share this level of detail since they were so seldom asked their opinion about anything.

Bracketing: This is used to ask about things that people might not want to share, at least initially during a conversation: age, pricing, revenue and cost. I often bracket when I am asking for a person's age, so we can include that demographic in our analysis. I tack this on at the very end when he is comfortable with me.

This was easy to get at the end of my conversation with the tradesmen, as by then we had built a rapport. Most of them gave me their actual age when all I was looking for was their age within a 10-year range!

Other Considerations

In competitive intelligence interviewing, you want to make sure you don't give away exactly what you're looking for. Your objective is to get answers to your questions, and I've found that indirect questions work well. However, depending on how and what you ask, you might reveal information you didn't intend to, such as your company's market development plans. Sometimes I plant camouflage questions in the mix to prevent giving myself away.

During any competitive intelligence conversation, you never give away your company's proprietary data.

Those are questions that we don't need answers to, that are interesting but off-topic. They keep the conversation flowing. You need to create your questions thoughtfully and be ready for unanticipated conversational flow by using decision tree thinking.

What Will You Share?

Conversation is a two-way street, not like interrogation, which is more of a one-way conversation where the interrogator is pumping for information from the other person.

During a competitive intelligence conversation, you never give away your company's proprietary data, notably what's in the pipeline for product development. You can, though, share public information that they might not know, and company information that salespeople tell customers and prospects. This keeps the other person's interest and boosts your credibility.

I have learned that I need to have enough nuggets to share during any conversation to keep the other person engaged without dominating the conversation. By the same token, I need to be prepared to answer the questions the other person might ask me. I try to think through what questions might be asked beforehand, so I have prepared answers in my mind.

In some cases, I have shared what I have learned about other competitors to get the conversation flowing. Sometimes he will correct me when he disagrees with what I've learned. Sometimes he is right.

As a final step, be specific about what you choose to share and what you choose not to share. Review your questions. Are they giving you away? When in doubt, it's good to check with your legal department but actually, even when not in doubt.

your turn

I challenge you to reword your next set of questions to be friendly to the person you'll be talking with. Once completed, reorder them from the open-ended, easy discussion items to more specific ones.

Consider the different ways the conversation might flow. Think about your response to the other person's questions. Be prepared for surprises!

Don't forget to think about what you want to share with the other person. This is a conversation, not an interrogation!

Next

- Reach out to that person and conduct your conversation.
- Do you notice the difference, just from this small amount of preparation?
- How did it go? What went well? What didn't?
- What did you learn from that person that you might not have without this preparation?
- What did you learn that you might try next time?

By failing to prepare
you are preparing to fail.

—**Benjamin Franklin**

chapter four

Plan:
Research: Warm Up
the Interview

The Collection Continuum

Focus on human conversation,
but the digital world is a great resource
to find and connect with people.

In this phase, you are looking for the right person or people to speak with. That's comparatively easy in a Win/Loss interview. You want to talk to the key contact at the customer's company. Most companies are not that large, although some of their customer relationship management systems make it hard to find the right contact person! When the customer works for a large company, they have a big sales team. The sale is complex, and you may be challenged to find the right person at the customer's company. You may also need to interview several people. But often enough in Win/Loss calls, you can easily find the key contact person for a conversation.

Let's consider a project where you don't know who you need to talk with to get the information that you need. I identify organizations who care about what I'm looking for. They're always out there. Then I look for people who work at them or who have recently left them. I might find that they're published and have written an article on what I'm looking for. I might talk to their competitors, our customers, their competitor's customers or our supply chain.

I also like to stay up on current events because a current event can often be an icebreaker, especially if you can't find something else you share in common to talk about.

Think about the small talk that you can develop. Here is a list of ideas to get you started:

- You have a friend or colleague in common.
- You have read an article about her company, its products, etc.
- You have read an article/blog she has written.
- You can discuss an industry trend or a new industry issue. (technology, regulation)
- You share a hometown in common.
- You have traveled to his hometown.
- You've worked or you work in the same industry.
- You've worked at his company.
- You've worked in her position at another company.
- You share a hobby.
- You support the same charity.
- You've gone to the same school or appreciate his education.
- You acknowledge challenges faced in her industry.
- You share a success story that engages him.

Be creative and you'll find your way into small talk. You just need one or two of these small talk items. If you indicate that you know too much about him, it could make him uncomfortable. My first choice is always a personal referral, but that is not always possible.

Decide how long you will engage with the person or people you need to talk to. Is it 15 or 30 minutes or are you just lucky if she gives you two minutes? Will this conversation be a set duration that both parties agree to? For example, he knows who you are, and you know who he is before you talk. He might be a peer you want to connect with, or perhaps an industry expert you dig up but don't know.

For those who are interested in the science behind building a good connection during a conversation, read Judith Glaser's book, *Conversational Intelligence: How Great Leaders Build Trust and Get Great Results.* Glaser says to focus on relationships first to connect with another person, which makes the other person feel like you're a friend. This signals the hypothalamus—also referred to as the heart brain—that it's safe to connect, and you can get in synch with the other person and build rapport.

You need to be open to digital sources and use them creatively. Be persistent.

Collection Continuum

Seena Sharp, retired CI professional and author of *Competitive Intelligence Advantage* shares,

> Good results require a good understanding of the business world and how it operates. Just knowing the industry is not sufficient, especially for ferreting

out those nuggets of insight and change that help
the company gain an advantage and grow.

When I take on a project, I consider the Collection Continuum.
I usually start with the Internet and go to social media before
talking to anyone. I go up and down the Collection Continuum
steps. Sometimes I read an industry report that initially makes
little sense to me. When I reread the industry report after talking
to an industry expert, it might make a lot more sense. Be flexible
and exploratory in your research.

Collection Continuum

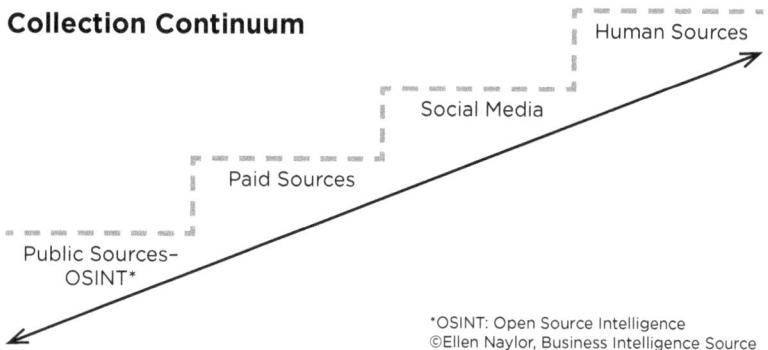

Human Sources

Social Media

Paid Sources

Public Sources–
OSINT*

*OSINT: Open Source Intelligence
©Ellen Naylor, Business Intelligence Source

The Internet, paid sources and social media are forever
evolving. You need to stay on top of this as a researcher. For
example, Threads came on board in 2023 as a competitor to X
after Elon Musk took ownership. Will Threads last? Remember
Google+? Now we have generative AI that I feel is changing
digital research almost daily.

Loosen Their Lips will not focus on many specific Internet and
social media sources–too many become outdated quickly. My focus
is on human conversation, but the digital world is a great resource
to find and connect with people. You need to be open to digital
sources and use them creatively. Be persistent.

Collection Continuum Case Study

CI professional Suki Fuller, CEO of Miribure, related a story about using pharmaceutical conferences to gather baseline information. Her story illustrates how she used the Collection Continuum.

> Before you go to the conference you would study the person and the pharmaceutical product online. For example, you would look at the targeted poster that would describe the pharmaceutical product online. A poster is a graphic presentation of an author's research, which includes photos or diagrams and some text, and is a snapshot, in this case of the pharmaceutical product. Usually, the online poster would not include a picture of the author, just her last name and first initial, and perhaps the university she was affiliated with.
>
> At the pharmaceutical conference you would see the author standing by her poster explaining prepared content about the poster. You'd learn what she looks like and her full name so you could find her on LinkedIn or some academic places where she would be talking in more detail about what her company was doing beyond what you learned at her poster session. You might even get to see her in a panel discussion where you might ask some questions at the end. You also glean some soft information about her.
>
> Then you might want to learn where she's been traveling. She might share that she's been to this cool conference but won't tell you which one it is. But then she posts a photo from the conference. It looks like

it's in Brisbane, but there is no conference going on there. You conclude that this pharmaceutical company is having a conference in Brisbane for its employees.

So, as you can see, you travel up and down the steps of the Collection Continuum, when looking for information about a person or product, and can piece together the information to forecast what's next!

your turn

Before your next important conversation, develop some small talk to get it started. How did it go? Did this help you get the other person to share more, sooner?

The purpose of information is not knowledge. It is being able to take the right action.

—**Peter Drucker,** Management Guru

chapter five

Plan:
Research: The Collection Continuum
Digital Sources

Most of the time, I prefer online paid sources
more than the open Internet since they have been curated.

Too many people skimp on digital research before conducting
interviews. You'll miss key connecting points if you don't do your
homework and then you'll waste a conversation opportunity.

Public and Paid Sources

I like Internet sources since they're cost-effective, convenient, quick
and a great way to build your knowledge, especially in an area
you're not familiar with. As I start a project, I think, "Who else
cares about or collects the information I'm looking for? Why and
where might it be available?"

You can use the Information Nodes model that CI professional
Amir Fleischman presents in his book, *Beating Competition through
Web Intelligence*. Fleischman divides online business information
sources into eight different categories below. In each of the categories—or nodes—the information you are looking for may be found.

- *Organizations*: unions, associations, corporations and any other body that possesses necessary information or knows where to obtain it

- *Industry events*: exhibitions, conferences, workshops, conventions and any event relevant to your project

- *Informal gatherings*: discussion groups, forums, communities and other online meetups

- *Databases*: portals, indexes, directories and lists of information items of various types

- *Written materials*: sources that are divided into three subcategories

    - *News: articles, essays, newsletters, blogs*

    - *Legal documents: lawsuits, proceedings, verdicts*

    - *Empirical information: reports, market research, reviews*

- *Experts*: consultants, writers, lecturers, committee members

- *Business information*: projects, price offers, contracts, tenders

- *Stakeholders:* people, businesses and companies

Most of the time I prefer online paid sources more than the open Internet since they have been curated. For example, it's helpful to read a Gartner report in a technical area that provides its perspective on an industry segment, a service provider comparison, and profiles of the industry segment's service providers. While the Gartner report is biased, if you work in tech, many industry players who you will talk with read Gartner reports and are influenced by its analysis and conclusions.

Accurate information is often buried in the volume of content.

I am also skeptical about the information I read on the Internet. Accurate information is often buried in the volume of content. Data can be inaccurate, outdated, biased, purposely deceitful, and often misses soft information aka human feelings and critical thinking. At a Special Libraries Association conference, Cynthia Lesky, President of Threshold Information, said that too much news comes from biased company press releases. Meanwhile, others take the biased company's press release, add their own spin and publish it. On the bright side, press releases can be a great reference point when you're looking to interview someone. They might include people you'd like to talk to.

Remember anything that you write on the Internet is a permanent digital record. Those you're going to interview can read up on you. That's also true for social media that is discussed next. All of it can be scraped in Generative AI.

Social Media

Social media has made it much easier to find people, although you need to have healthy skepticism since some people are self-proclaimed experts who might not be. Presently, I use LinkedIn more than any other platform to find businesspeople. I was an early adopter, so I have many connections and followers. This is a huge benefit to find people without paying for LinkedIn's Navigator. Who knows what will emerge next to help us find businesspeople so easily?

LinkedIn Case Study

I needed an expert who was knowledgeable about a company. I used LinkedIn to locate him. I was researching a company to learn how it was structured and how it operated. I had done significant digital research and wanted to talk to a senior leader who had been with the company for a while. I found just the person through LinkedIn. He was based in Texas and provided his telephone number and invited calls from his LinkedIn profile. Typically, Texans are very friendly. This person was no exception. We spoke for about an hour, and I got all the information I needed from a reliable source.

I've also used LinkedIn to put together organizational charts of smaller, privately held companies. LinkedIn is a great way to learn about a company's hiring practices: average age of employees, turnover, etc. Granted, it's not totally accurate as it is self-reported by each individual. However, as of this writing, it's better than most other sources for finding business contacts.

Social Media from the Experts

OSINT, also known as open-source intelligence, and social media expert Amir Fleischman advises that social media networks tend to reveal "behind the scenes" information that is not indexed by search engines as often as formal websites. Numerous valuable unstructured data may help you form an accurate profile of a potentially threatening competitor. Or, it might share that a key strategic customer has a birthday today.

You are manipulated through your experience on these platforms that can change how you think and how you behave.

Whenever it comes to social media intelligence (SOCMINT), you should also follow your target's followers. Who knows, they may eventually end up as your customers. Social media is full of names, pictures, videos, and what targets and followers are after. Take advantage of that and use it wisely.

CI professional Suki Fuller complains that many people don't even do a web search before meeting people. It's such a gold mine!

Type the name of the person and learn what he looks like. Even if his Instagram account is locked, you get to see his profile picture. It's quite telling since it's a personal photo, not the business image in LinkedIn or X. If he is on Facebook, it can be telling on the personal side, which can be handy for when you meet face-to-face. And there is always TikTok, the fastest-growing social media player in 2024. The person might have a video presence on YouTube or Vimeo. There are so many places to look and over time there will be even more! Use social media to construct a profile of the person you'll be speaking with.

I love how Fuller used social media to learn which physicians (and where) were associated with clinical trials for a pharmaceutical company. This was early in social media days, and it was an amazing find!

Some of the company executives were on top of what was hip and hot back then. They were using Foursquare as they checked into various Starbucks across the US. Fuller had a list of all the locations for clinical trials by specific therapeutic area. If they were going to visit an office or lab where a doctor was working in a therapeutic area, they would check in at the local Starbucks. Their post would include all the metadata in their pictures: the location, the time and the coordinates. Let's say the executive checked in at a Starbucks in Hoboken, New Jersey, next to a clinical trial location. Bingo, Fuller learned that this doctor was working on the cardiovascular clinical trial that she was researching.

Beware!

Know that search engines, news sites, Amazon and social media are deliberately designed algorithmically to use your preferences to selectively show you items in your feed. You are fed tailored, computer curated content that becomes familiar and thus reinforces your preferences for future clicks. Thus, you are manipulated through your experience on these platforms that can change how you think and how you behave. I fear this will become even worse with generative AI.

One way to counter this trap aside from incognito searching, is to connect with people who do not share your ethnicity or your beliefs. Judson Brewer expresses this in *Unwinding Anxiety*. The ambiguity to consider several facts or opinions that might be conflicting is challenging. This feels less secure than the ingroup feel, a shared view or one from a single perspective that you get from social media when you just follow like-minded people. That is a growing blind spot many of us have. We have become so polarized as a global society that it spills into research and decision-making. The feedback on social media is binary and quantitative, with numbers of likes and retweets. This compares to the risk and fear people have around reading body language and interpreting tone of voice during in-person or video conversations, especially with people who don't share your views.

Generative AI

The Wall Street Journal article "AI in Process Automation" on November 13, 2023, stated, "The extraordinary promise of AI is driving a profound transformation in the world of business technology." Its capacity to analyze data, automate tasks and augment human decision-making is a great opportunity to spur growth, efficiency and innovation for companies, particularly for knowledge workers and IT professionals.

Generative AI is hot and it's hard to predict how much it's going to change research, except that it already has and will continue as the technology is further developed. Presently, it saves a lot of time when conducting digital research, writing it up and ideating. Generative AI has its limitations and needs to be checked for accuracy just like any source. Sometimes the results are garbage referred to as hallucination. The sources behind AI are mostly the Internet and social media. Companies can also include internal sources such as company-generated content, industry reports and other paid sources. Generative AI will alter the Collection Continuum and perhaps make it defunct.

In 2023, a friend told me that he forgot that he was not having a conversation with a human when he used generative AI. This was before generative AI had evolved into video as it does presently. A generative AI digital or video dialogue is **not** with a human. Yet, Generative AI is crossing more into the territory of data collection and interaction that was previously only possible by talking to another person, and analysis that was previously only conducted by humans. I think it's fair to project that Generative AI might not replace you as a conversationalist, but a person who uses Generative AI could if you refuse to use it.

Remember, generative AI does not have a soul, empathy, judgment or fundamental innovation. But Generative AI is taking you to places where you couldn't go even one year ago. And that trend is only going to continue and perhaps accelerate. I think those who embrace and use Generative AI will free up their time to do more work that adds value, and allows them to tap into their imagination, creativity, problem-solving and critical thinking. Generative AI will free up time to be better communicators with humans! Will you value human interaction more or less as a result? Or will you just use more generative AI at the expense of human communication? How well will you adopt and adapt to generative AI? It is coming at us so quickly!

According to Chris Inglis, the US government's first national cyber director, the pace of change in technology is what boards need to pay attention to. "The interesting thing about ChatGPT isn't what it is at the moment, but the speed at which it's come at us, and perhaps, what might come at us in the next few weeks, not years," Inglis said. And ChatGPT has plenty of competition!

Some issues remain in these early days of generative AI and more will emerge as generative AI advances.

- How can companies fully leverage the capabilities of generative AI while preserving the privacy and security of the data that fuels it? How will it be regulated?

- What about all the energy that is required to fuel Generative AI?

- Like many technical advances, Generative AI has replaced jobs and will continue to do so. What new opportunities will open up? Where will those displaced people find training and employment?

- Will companies be open to hiring or rehiring some of the displaced employees if they realize that generative AI isn't as effective as they thought?

**Without data,
you're just another person
with an opinion.**
—W. Edwards Deming

chapter six

Plan:
Research: The Collection
Continuum:
Human Sources

You build trust one person at a time.

I value human sources due to my extensive experience and success from talking to people to get answers. Digital feedback often obscures the view of feelings and actions toward others. Talking to people reduces the silos and blind spots you get from relying solely on Internet and social media research.

My decades working in competitive intelligence have reinforced my belief that humans are the best source of information through an analog, real-time dialog whether on a video, audio call or in-person conversation. You get sharpness and depth of information that is seldom available through online sources. Talking to a human extends your reach and builds up your social capital. You build trust one person at a time.

In my experience most people want to help. All you have to do is ask. They can connect you to their people network and refer you to so many more sources, but there is a drawback. Talking to humans is time-consuming and can be expensive if you're outsourcing this.

If you're cold calling, good luck. Most people don't answer their phones unless you're in their e-directory. So, you must get on the other person's calendar. Even then, sometimes they don't show up at the agreed time. You might connect with the wrong people for what you need, even though they've been referred to you by trustworthy, well-meaning colleagues. So, you're back to the drawing board.

You're depending on the skill of the interviewer when talking to humans. It's subjective and requires the most fluid of skills. There is also a margin of error. For example, the interviewer can miss cues or fail to build rapport. He might not be good at detecting deception, so he could be fed false or misleading information, and not realize or challenge it.

You also have ethical issues to consider when conducting a conversation. Chapter 7, *Prepare Your Introduction and Ethics,* will create a guide for you. People also lie ... sometimes on purpose. Sometimes they don't really know but being helpful want to tell you something. Chapter 18, *Execute: Deception, Misinformation, Omission,* will be an eye-opener.

Everyone is in such a hurry to get information. The fastest way I know to get information about your competition and their products is to attend an industry trade show or conference. Almost everyone who is presenting or exhibiting is in the sales and marketing mode and wants to tell you about his products or services, including what is in his company's pipeline. Exhibitors often show product demos. Consultants and industry experts also attend and share what they know. But sometimes you need to get answers sooner, and the conference isn't for another six months.

Friendlies

Great minds don't think alike.
They challenge each other to think differently.
—**Adam Grant,** Organizational Psychologist and Professor

Jonathan Calof, CI Professor at the University of Ottawa, talks
about Friendlies in his book, *Gaining Market Insight from Events:
A Lifetime Journey*. I like to find Friendlies for any project I'm
working on. Friendlies are people who help me get what I'm looking
for, even if it's just a step along the way. Since I'm a consultant
they all work outside of my company.

Below are some sources for you to consider outside of your
company!

External Competitive Intelligence Sources

Customers and Churns
Suppliers and Partners
Competitor's Customers
Consultants
Regulators
Recruiters
Unions
Association Members
Think Tanks
Reporters Journalists
Technical Experts
Ad Agencies
Engineers Researchers
Professors

*Find Friendlies
Outside Your Company*

© Ellen Naylor, Business
Intelligence Source

You need to assess the reliability and validity of your
Friendlies. The next page lists questions I think about to evaluate
the quality and perspective of my Friendlies. Knowledge sharing

and strong responsiveness help me stay focused on the most helpful Friendlies. Helpful can also mean they're part of what Professor Adam Grant refers to as your challenge network. These people challenge your thinking in that they bring up points you might not be aware of or agree with, which is invaluable.

Gauging Friendlies

- How responsive is this person when you reach out? (digitally, mobile, video or in-person)

- Does he get back to you in a timely fashion?

- Is she an effective communicator?

- What is the quality of his knowledge sharing? Subject matter expertise?

- Is it commonly known or less well-known knowledge that he shares?

- Do you have reciprocal working knowledge or is it one way?

- How valuable are his people sharing and contact leads?

- Is she a critical thinker? Does she offer insight?

- Is she highly regarded by someone in your network? Who and why?

- If not, how did you connect with her?

- Does he meet your ethical standards?

Friendlies: Internal Sources

Over the years I've been told that 80% of what you need to know can be found by those working at your company. Don't forget some of the best Friendlies work at your company. You need to find out who they are and build relationships. In many cases, you can help them too. After all, mutual benefit is key!

Below are a few sources to connect with at your company!

Find Friendlies in Your Company

Find Friendlies in Your Company

Customer Success & Tech Support

Sales and Sales Enablement

Marketing and Operations

(UX) User Experience Help Desk

Product Managers

Product Marketing

Research and Development

Admins and Executives

Finance and Accounting

Strategic Planning

Purchasing and HR

Legal and Security

PR & Investor Relations

Corporate Communications

© Ellen Naylor, Business Intelligence Source

Case Study: Friendlies

Andrew Beurschgens, Senior Insight Manager of CI, shared how connecting with frontline employees within his telco company was a goldmine. He was working on a project for a member of the management team who managed customer service. While the business was winning in the market it served, the Customer Service Director was not keen to start asking questions after the momentum had stopped. The focus areas of how it was doing, what it was doing, and why in the call center environment, were very difficult to source without people from the frontline.

The Customer Service Project Coordinator shared that a few colleagues had worked at the company Andrew was investigating. Call center employees moved between call centers from competing brands when they were located in the same area. Andrew reached out to them copying both the Project Coordinator and the Customer Service Director identifying who he was, and what he was looking to achieve without breaching any nondisclosure agreements they might have signed with their former employer.

Andrew traveled to the call center and met the new recruits in one-on-one meetings to explore the issues and to understand what was next for the competitor's customer service area. He spent a day amassing their insights into the issues he was exploring to a depth and understanding beyond his, the Project Coordinator and the Customer Service Director. He shared his notes about the issues with the Project Coordinator and the Customer Service Director copying the new recruits.

Andrew concluded that reaching out and meeting the frontline colleagues, who had experienced life from both brands' perspectives, allowed for the rich understanding to facilitate the project's excellent outcome. It complemented the work undertaken by the agency partnered on this project. It was shared with the agency to increase their credibility with the sources they had connected with as well.

You'll also note that Andrew was ethical in making sure that those he spoke to were not breaching any nondisclosure agreements. He was also good at communicating and sharing with the right people as he conducted the research, even at the end by sharing with the ad agency. This is how you build social capital! Andrew is rich in social capital.

your turn

Who are your Friendlies? Why?

Internal company Friendlies?

External company Friendlies?

Do you qualify Friendlies by expertise? Industry? Geography? Culture? Issues? Politics?

Who are members of your challenge network? If you don't have a challenge network, find them.

The Information Spiral

I learned about The Information Spiral diagram from my intelligence world colleagues. I love it since it helps me organize who I want to talk to from the least important or peripheral sources all the way to talking directly to the competitor's company. You can organize this for any project you're working on.

Following the information spiral on the following page, I would start by focusing on ex-customers who've gone to the competition as well as our company's customers who considered the competitor in a recent bid but

> **I build my knowledge base with each conversation.**

chose us. Then I'd target government sources, industry associations, the competitor's ex-employees, suppliers, trade unions and distributors. Lastly, I would reach out to the competitor that I call the target company.

The Information Spiral

Ex-
Employees

Trade
Unions   Customers

Suppliers

Target
Company   Ex-Customers

Distributors
Associations

Government

© Ellen Naylor, Business
Intelligence Source

What's great is you can use The Information Spiral to create an Organizational Contact Sheet. I usually will start with someone who is less important for each source category, so I can flesh out a good approach, and see which questions flow nicely in conversation. I will change or adapt my questions depending on who I am talking to, and what gaps of information remain.

Organizational Contact Sheet

Sources	Name	Title	Company	How Connected	Date 1st Contacted	Date 2nd Time	Date 3rd Time
1. Ex-Customers							
2. Customers							
3. Govt Sources							
4. Industry Associates							
5. Ex-Employees							
6. Suppliers							
7. Trade Unions							
8. Distributors							
9. Competitors							

CI professional Melanie Prudom says, "You learn as you go." She also reminds us that when you adapt your questions as you get further into collection, you get to more of the unknown space. Whether you're in competitive intelligence or another field doing research, you're looking for insight, and that often comes from what you didn't even know to ask about.

I build my knowledge base with each conversation so that by the time I reach the most important people for my project, I've learned enough to be dangerous. I can also use the information I've learned from earlier conversations to probe more deeply. Talking to a variety of people also helps me verify the quality of my data.

Although this isn't part of planning, I add every person I speak with to my contact database from the Organizational Contact Sheet. You never know when you'll want to reach out to them again. You also never know when they might reach out to you. Keeping track of all these people also adds to your social capital. I've introduced people to each other who wouldn't have met except through my connection. It feels great to help people.

your turn

I challenge you to develop an Information Spiral and Organizational Contact Sheet for your next project! Be creative: you can use these tools to improve your job-hunting efforts or move your way down the sales funnel.

Where else would you like to use them?

You have to believe in yourself.

—**Sun Tzu,** Chinese Philosopher

chapter seven

Plan:
Prepare Your
Introduction and Ethics

Be flexible in your approach and
don't take yourself too seriously.

When thinking about your introduction, consider what's in it
for the other person to share with you. What do you think his
attitude will be about sharing? Is confidentiality an issue that you
need to bring up?

I always introduce myself at the start of the call. Usually the
call is not cold, as I've set up a video call. I thank him for taking
the time to speak with me. Assuming he does not have a gruff tone
of voice, I might ask how he's doing as one often does. Then we
get on with the business of the call.

Remember it's more about how kind and confident you
come across than crafting the exact words you will use in your
introduction. This reality was a game-changer for me. Suddenly,
I became less nervous about my introduction and no longer practiced my introductory words. I want to come across as confident
and to believe that the other person will cooperate with me.

Another game-changer: Don't take yourself too seriously. Be creative and have fun.

In one project I was helping a healthcare company determine its opportunity to develop a product that hospitals would use. We needed to assess the company's potential customers' needs. The client gave me a list of people to call from a healthcare association. I got through to about 20 of them, but I needed to speak to another 20 people.

I panicked. Where else could I find the right people to talk to? How would I introduce myself to them? The introduction I had used with the leads from the association would not work. Then I thought to contact hospitals since they would be the customers for this product. What's the worst thing that would happen, I wondered? I could blow the call and simply try another hospital. That's not a big deal. Next, I needed to figure out which hospital department would use this product, and what hospitals called that department. I found out it varied by hospital and the switchboard operators helped me as they directed my call to the right area.

So, I had three introductions to make: one to the switchboard operator; one to the person who I was transferred to; and a third to the senior person in the department. In all cases, my introduction was short, and I was confident that the senior hospital worker would tell me what I needed

It's important that you maintain integrity in terms of how you get the information you seek.

since this product would make her life easier. Most of them questioned why I was doing this research, which I was prepared to answer. I was pleasantly surprised by how friendly everyone was. I learned that they were happy to share what I was looking for as long as I was quick. I think my attitude enabled this outcome. I was flexible in my approach and didn't take myself too seriously. My anxiety level was greatly reduced once I thought to connect with hospitals.

Ethics

> When I do good, I feel good.
> When I do bad, I feel bad and that's my religion.
> **—Abraham Lincoln**

Let's bring ethics into planning a conversation. It applies in every phase of competitive intelligence collection. Whatever you do, it's important that you maintain integrity in terms of how you get the information you seek.

I have learned that I need to tell the other person enough about myself so he feels comfortable sharing with me. I need to gain his trust, and the sooner the better.

One size doesn't fit all. Some people don't want to hear much about me, so I don't tell them. Meanwhile others ask multiple questions, almost testing me. I must answer them satisfactorily before we can get to the conversation I want to have.

If someone asks who you are and where you work, don't misrepresent yourself. Be honest and tell them. If they decide not to continue the conversation, you can usually find someone else. I have only had one person discontinue a conversation in my 40+ years of interviewing, and that was 20 minutes into the conversation.

Cold calls are rare these days. You don't have to divulge who you are right away in a cold call, especially if the other person doesn't ask. These days, most of the time I have emailed or texted the other person an invitation to have a conversation.

Have empathy. Put yourself in the other person's shoes as best you can. He might have had some bad experiences being interviewed or having a conversation like the one you're proposing. Perhaps he felt betrayed. Maybe she is having a bad day, and your conversation is sandwiched in between unpleasant events. You never know what burdens other people are carrying. But you know that you need to quickly develop a certain amount of trust and rapport with the other person to get her to tell you what you're looking for.

Ethics Case Studies
Ethics also carries into the information you gather. How much is OK to share with your client? In one extreme experience, I asked the competitor for a representative sample of its customers. The person on the other end, ever helpful, was a temporary employee. She sent me four pages, single-spaced, which included **all** the competitive company's customers. I picked about 20 customers to share with my client.

In another instance, I negotiated with a consulting firm to get a few hours of conversation for our mutual client. While the consulting firm had a contract with my client, they didn't have one with me. I asked what I could provide them with to get a few hours of their time. They wanted pricing from a telco provider that they'd been unable to get. Surprisingly, I lucked out. In one phone call I got this data. A temporary employee sent me all the telco's pricing data. Again, this was too much to share with the consulting firm. But I shared enough to get a few hours to pick their brains.

These two stories also illustrate the risk of hiring temporary employees in public-facing positions. These two people were just being helpful, and didn't ask why I wanted the information, who it was for or how it would be used.

Consultant Ethics

As a consultant, I get hired to conduct conversations that are better done by a third party such as Win/Loss, retention and churn interviews. Sometimes companies hire consultants to use underhanded means to gain competitive intelligence. Or they hire consultants and tell us we can't talk to the competitor, and they're looking for the competitor's pipeline that no one else would know.

I was hired to do a trade show collection at the Neocon, a huge commercial furniture conference held in the Merchandise Mart in Chicago. My client suggested that I represent myself as an employee of a large company so their competitors would divulge more. I told my client that I only work using my own name and company name. They hired me knowing this. As it turned out, I visited the key competitor's exhibit showroom with a large software company, so hit the jackpot. I was new to this space and had lots of questions. They had better ones and their attentive salesperson answered them well. My client was thrilled with the results.

Another unethical practice that I turn down is when clients want me to issue a request for proposal (RFP) to get detailed pricing from their competitors. Not only is this unethical, but it's also unkind. I am not going to get a salesperson's hopes up for a sale when it's a hoax. Having come from Sales, I know from experience how many hours are consumed to answer an RFP.

There are instances where I have turned down work because my prospective client was looking for information that is ALL proprietary information. Not only is this difficult to get, but it is unethical to go after it.

Recording Conversations

Some colleagues in the technology business have told me they assume that every conversation is being recorded. This is another ethical consideration. Can you record calls without telling the other person? The answer is yes and no in the US.

In most states only one party needs to consent to record the conversation, so that can be you. In other states you must get consent from the other person to legally record your conversation. If the other person doesn't agree, then you are breaking the law if you record the call. The states that currently require two-party consent are California, Delaware, Florida, Illinois, Maryland, Massachusetts, Montana, Nevada, New Hampshire, Pennsylvania and Washington.

If you want to record a call with a European colleague, you must abide by the General Data Protection Regulation (GDPR) guidelines. You must inform the other person if you're recording a call, including why.

For businesses recording telephone calls under GDPR, you must meet specific criteria:

1. *Transparency:* Inform participants that the phone conversation is being recorded and state the purpose clearly.

2. *Secure Storage:* Use encrypted systems to protect recordings from unauthorized access or breaches.

3. *Retention Periods:* Keep recordings only as long as necessary and securely delete them after their purpose has been fulfilled.

The bottom line is you must learn and abide by the law about recording your conversation depending on where you are located!

Conclusions

We tread a fine line in competitive intelligence. We look for what's not public information by talking to people in the know. We also note patterns of what's relevant in the competitive market we're researching. We're good at putting things together and making intelligent guesses based on what we dig up on the Internet, social media and through conversations. In addition, most of us have strong intuitive skills and are critical thinkers, which helps us direct our companies to think more creatively about the future.

Ethics is an individual thing. You must decide what you are comfortable with during these conversations. You also need to be aware of legal boundaries. Each customer and each industry's ethics vary. But if you do something that you know is unethical, you are not going to feel good about yourself. You may also damage your reputation, which would be difficult to recover from.

The Council of Competitive Intelligence Fellows has good ethical guidelines. *www.cifellows.com/about-us/ethics/*. So does the Strategic Consortium of Intelligence Professionals (SCIP) formerly the Strategic Competitive Intelligence Professionals: *www.scip.org/page/Ethical-Intelligence.*

You need to develop your own code of ethics. Ask your company if it has a code of ethics as many do these days. If not, offer to help your company's legal staff draft one. If you're consulting, ask the company who hired you if it abides by a code of ethics. This is also a great way to find out how the company does business and if you want to do business with the company.

Oprah Winfrey sums up personal ethics nicely: "Real integrity is doing the right thing, knowing that nobody is going to know whether you did it or not."

your turn

How do you prepare your introductions for conversations?

I challenge you to act more confidently and believe you'll get what you're looking for during your next conversation. How did it go?

Don't take yourself too seriously!

Be ethical: You must live with yourself and how you are.

Write your personal code of ethics.

chapter eight

Pre-Execution: Get Grounded

What's the **best** thing
that will happen during this conversation?

The first phase of conversation: Plan. Focus on determining your goals, conducting the research and developing the questions to achieve your goals. Pre-Execution focuses on the next stage, getting yourself psychologically and emotionally prepared to handle a conversation. The focus here is on various ways to get grounded, build self-knowledge and assess the motivation of the person you'll speak with to maximize his sharing.

You want to come across in a conversation as a likable, confident person who expects the other person to be cooperative. One way to do this is to get grounded before the conversation. For many years I didn't do this. I spent my time nervously rehearsing my introduction and rewording the questions.

Getting grounded before important conversations was a breakthrough for me: not just for competitive intelligence conversations, but also for sales calls and challenging conversations in my professional and personal life. My husband, Rodgers, gets grounded before his art shows, and repeatedly during those long days when he wants to stay on top of his game with good energy for art lovers and customers who visit his booth.

Getting grounded helps you stay focused on what you'd like to accomplish during a conversation. Many people experience fear when thinking about the outcome of a conversation.

Psych yourself up and think: What's the **worst** thing that will happen during this conversation?

The worst things are:

- She doesn't cooperate.

- He is not the knowledgeable source you thought he'd be.

- He is having a bad day and takes it out on you.

- She hangs up on you (if you're on your phone).

None of these sounds too scary to me and I've experienced all these and more. The worst thing for me is when he ignores my outreach, so I don't get to have a conversation.

Now really psych yourself up and think: What's the **best** thing that will happen during this conversation?

- Do you visualize success? Envision and expect the person to share with you.

- What does success look like?

- What does success feel like?

Thinking in this positive way and visualizing success makes me smile and boosts my spirits.

There are many ways to get grounded: meditation, prayer, breathing exercises and Amy Cuddy's Power Pose. I will describe a few of these to help you decide how you'd like to get grounded. I get grounded in different ways depending on the situation I'm facing, how I'm feeling, and how much time I have to get grounded before the conversation.

Meditation

First keep the peace within yourself,
then you can also bring peace to others.
—Thomas A. Kempis, Augustinian Monk, author of *Imitation of Christ*

Guided meditation is a good place to start if you're new to meditation. It helps me think more clearly, cleans my mind of cluttering thoughts, and slows incessant thinking. It takes me to a state of mindfulness. Dr. Jon Kabat-Zinn defines mindfulness as, "The awareness that arises when paying attention in the present moment on purpose nonjudgmentally." Being mindful through meditation is an effective way to get yourself grounded and focused before an important conversation. You start by focusing on your breath: the in breath and the out breath.

Guided meditation can range from a few minutes to an hour depending on what you decide to do. There is silent meditation for those who appreciate going to their own quiet space. Others find that chanting or repeating one word while meditating is relaxing and helps them get focused.

There are numerous apps for meditation, both guided and silent. One of my favorite meditations is from Plum Village. This is a Buddhist practice founded by the Zen Monastic, Thích Nhất Hạnh, referred to as the Father of Mindfulness. Plum Village's app is free and offers many guided and silent meditations in multiple languages. I attended a Plum Village class entitled Zen and the Art of Saving the Planet, also the title of a book by Thích Nhất Hạnh.

Insight Timer is a free meditation app. It claims to be the number one app for sleep, anxiety and stress with many choices for meditation and calming talks. As of this writing, Insight Timer has the world's largest library of free guided meditations with 300,000 titles in 50 languages from psychologists, spiritual leaders and mindfulness teachers. It also offers yoga music and classes. Calm and Headspace are competing apps.

I like to do silent meditation while doing mundane tasks like washing the dishes, cleaning our house or folding the laundry. My favorite silent meditation activity is walking in our Denver neighborhood, but better yet in Colorado's Rocky Mountains or on a sandy beach anywhere. I find that meditating over time has somehow made me calmer, happier and more focused. You benefit the most from doing meditation every day, not just before an important conversation.

Breathing Exercises

According to the Mayo Clinic, a US medical research clinic, there is sufficient evidence to suggest that intentional breathing can calm and regulate the autonomic nervous system. The autonomic nervous system regulates involuntary body functions like temperature. It can lower blood pressure and provide an almost-immediate sense of calm and improve your mood.

There are numerous breathing exercises on the Insight Timer app. One I really like is Box Breathing. Here is a video you can watch: *https://bit.ly/3Ydsw3Q.* Box Breathing is used by the US military. It's comprised of a 4-count for all the steps of breathing, so it's easy to do. It's also very effective at getting you focused.

Box Breathing

Sit upright and slowly exhale all the oxygen out of your lungs. Focus on this and be conscious of what you're doing.

1. Inhale slowly and deeply through your nose to the count of four. Feel the coolness of the air you're breathing in and the way it fills your lungs, one section at a time until they're completely full.

2. Hold your breath for another slow count of four.

3. Exhale through your mouth for the same slow count of four, expelling the air from your lungs and abdomen. Be conscious of the feeling of the warm air leaving your lungs.

4. Hold your breath for another four counts and repeat the entire process again (1-4). If you have trouble clearing your thoughts, try humming in your mind or focus on counting.

In summary, you're slowly counting to four continuously during this deep breathing exercise as follows:

1. 4-count inhale through your nose

2. 4-count hold

3. 4-count exhale through your mouth

4. 4-count hold

A great breathing technique to reduce stress quickly is the Physiological Sigh.

The science behind this is that it balances the sympathetic and parasympathetic parts of your nervous system. It can help clear your mind while making you feel energized yet calm. It can also be used when you're not stressed but just want to boost your energy level. But to improve your conversation quality, this is a great breathing exercise to help you feel more present, grounded and at ease. You want to do Box Breathing for four to six breathing cycles. If the count of four is too much use three. Conversely, if the count of four is too easy, increase your count.

A great breathing technique to reduce stress quickly is the Physiological Sigh. Dr. Huberman, a professor of neurobiology and ophthalmology at Stanford University, explains the science and illustrates it here: *https://binged.it/46fYn7X* You inhale deeply once followed by a second shallow inhale, and then a long exhale. Do it one, two or three times. It works.

If you really want to geek out on understanding the physical and emotional benefits of breathing as well as how specific breathing techniques work, listen to Dr. Huberman's podcast, "How to Breathe Correctly for Optimal Health, Mood, Learning & Performance." *http://tinyurl.com/2vn6u3bk* He explains the biology behind breathing in great detail and then gets into breathing techniques. Warning: it's long! I liked the last one and one-half hours the best.

Dr. Andrew Weil's 4-7-8 Breathing Exercise
Another breathing exercise I like is Dr. Andrew Weil's 4-7-8 breathing technique. Watch it on YouTube here: *https://bit.ly/3tCx5qL.*

Sit upright and close your eyes. Clear the air out of your lungs through your mouth then close it.

1. Take a deep breath in through your nose quietly to a count of four.

2. Hold it for a count of seven.

3. Breathe out audibly and forcefully through your mouth

to a count of eight. (I like to say shhh as I breath out.)

4. Repeat this for four breath cycles.

Dr. Weil says this is a practice and you must do this at least twice a day. After a month you can increase to eight breath cycles, but that's the maximum he recommends.

It may take four to six weeks to get the full effect from this breathing exercise. Dr. Weil claims this practice will lower your heart rate, your blood pressure and improve blood circulation. It's the most effective anti-anxiety technique that he knows of.

Sometimes I use Dr. Weil's breathing exercise before doing a silent meditation.

Quick Grounding Methods

Amy Cuddy: Power Pose

In 2010, social psychologist Amy Cuddy along with Dana Carney and Andy Tap published the results of an experiment on how nonverbal expressions of power (such as expansive, open, space-occupying postures) affect people's feelings, behaviors and hormone levels. They concluded that adopting body postures associated with dominance and power—Power Posing—for as little as two minutes can increase testosterone levels by 20% and lower the stress hormone cortisol by about 25%. This is the science behind the Power Pose. They concluded that if you act powerfully, even if you don't feel powerful, you will begin to think powerfully.

Cuddy's June 2012 TED talk, "Your Body Language May Shape Who You Are" is the second most viewed TED Talk with more than 74 million views as of this writing. It is available here: *www.bit.ly/458gr26*.

She said not only does body language affect how others see us, but it may also change how we see ourselves. Cuddy argued that Power Posing—standing in a posture of confidence, even when we don't feel confident—can boost feelings of confidence and might improve our chances for success. Or as Cuddy says, "Fake it until you make it. Fake it until you become it."

- Your bodies can change your minds.

- Your minds can change your behavior.

- Your behavior changes your outcomes.

In 2015, Cuddy authored the best-selling book *Presence: Bringing Your Boldest Self to Your Biggest Challenges*. It built on the value of the outward practice of Power Posing to focus on projecting your authentic self with the inward-focused concept of presence defined as, "believing and trusting yourself—your real honest feelings, values and beliefs."

I use the practice of Power Posing before important conversations or public speaking engagements such as sales calls, customer calls, presentations, workshops, webinars and trade show collection projects. I may escape into the restroom if I'm in a public place or Power Pose in my hotel room before giving a presentation or workshop. I'll even do it during a workshop break to boost my energy and spirits.

your turn

I challenge you to make time to get grounded before a conversation.

How will you get grounded before conversations?

Experiment: Which grounding technique(s) works best for you?

How does your mood affect which technique you select?

How does the potential challenge of a conversation guide how you get grounded?

What other grounding techniques will you discover? Yoga, Tai Chi, prayer, etc.

What we think, feel, say to ourselves and others, and believe to be true creates our reality.

—**Tricia Molloy,** Work-Life Balance Speaker

chapter nine

Pre-Execution: Set Your Intention

If your peers and clients don't believe,
trust and respect you, you won't have staying power.

Effective communication hinges on the intention behind your words. Focus on being helpful rather than allowing emotions to dictate your responses. Benjamin Franklin said, "Speak not but what may benefit others or yourself." This underscores the importance of intention in communication. Emphasizing helpfulness can lead to a more productive conversation.

Dr. Amit Sood, CEO of the Global Center of Resilience and Wellbeing, suggests that for two seconds you align your heart with the other person without judgment and send him a silent, "I wish you well."

In a similar vein, I like to set a broad intention for my conversation beyond what I'm hoping to find out. This has been another quantum leap for me. My intention is very simple: I want the person I'm speaking with to feel better about himself when we say goodbye than when we said hello.

Here are some other intentions to consider:

• I want to share and learn from her wisdom.

- I am open to what he shares and to changing my assumptions and opinions.

- I will listen to him closely and without judgment.

- I will remain curious and polite even if she is rude to me.

The bottom line is you want to make the other person feel good about herself. People who you make feel good about themselves are more apt to like you. People share more with people they like.

You know you're doing something right when the other person thanks you at the end of a conversation that you initiated. And better yet, when he opens the door for you to get back with him.

You can't control others' attitudes about yourself, but you can control your own attitudes and behaviors.

I was so surprised the first time this happened some 20 years ago. It was a cold call. I wanted to learn how this man was using an electric measuring instrument. It was not an unusual conversation. But at the end of the call, he thanked me for calling and offered to help me should I need more information.

Remember, you leave an emotional trail behind. Consciously or unconsciously, you impact those around you whether you speak with them or are simply present listening to them. I love this sign from Indiana University Health:

> Please take responsibility for the energy you bring into this space. Your words matter. Your behaviors matter. Take a slow, deep breath and make sure your energy is in-check before entering. Thank you.

This is a simple way of thinking about how we impact people during a conversation. It's more than just our words.

Cooperative Intelligence

> Cooperation is the thorough conviction that
> nobody can get there unless everybody gets there.
>
> —**Virginia Burden,** *The Princess of Intuition*

Cooperative intelligence practices and attitudes positively influence your conversations! I started writing about cooperative intelligence in 2006. I was concerned that society was relying on digital communication too much and too often when making important decisions. This was before social media, Slack and texting became so prevalent, not to mention artificial intelligence. I wanted to emphasize the importance of human connection, which is the backbone of a competitive intelligence program … and so much else!

You can have the most effective processes in place and be the most intelligent, analytical, insightful and strategic person who delivers a stream of products. However, if your peers and clients don't believe, trust and respect you, you won't have staying power.

You can't control others' attitudes about yourself, but you can control your own attitudes and behaviors. Your attitude sets the tone regardless of the other person's motivation or status. You can project a positive attitude as one who provides a valuable service, intellectual capital and great connections. That's the backbone of cooperative intelligence.

Cooperative Leadership

> The person who sends out positive thoughts activates the world
> around him positively and draws back to himself positive results.
>
> —**Norman Vincent Peale**

Regardless of where you sit in your company, you are a leader. Before you can lead or motivate others to cooperate with you, reflect on how you lead yourself. Motivation is often triggered by your good example. What leaders do indicate more about who they are than what they say.

Cooperative leaders are not full of ego and don't push their own agendas. They welcome information from fellow employees and from colleagues outside their company. Employees and colleagues know a cooperative leader listens and will share information and make recommendations to improve the company's competitive position.

Cooperative Networking

Cooperative networking is the Win/Win of relationship building, one person at a time.

—Ellen Naylor

You develop your network by finding ways to help others. Conversation is an important steppingstone. You are helped because you help others with no strings attached. Instead of focusing on self-interest, you seek the common good. Years ago, Donna Fisher remarked on the boomerang effect when help arrives without explicit requests. Like a boomerang, the help you give comes back to you though often in a roundabout way.

Cooperative intelligence encompasses emotional intelligence and appreciative inquiry. Many companies do not take advantage of learning based on interviewing customers when they win significant business or have a great customer relationship. Competitive intelligence managers are often so critical that you don't seize the opportunity to build on your company's strengths in pursuit of the competition. Wouldn't Sales respond better to the positive approach of appreciative inquiry, "How will we improve market penetration in this industry?" versus the more critical approach of, "We're losing share in this industry. What are we doing wrong?"

Cooperative Communication

60% of all business problems stem from faulty communication.

—**Peter Drucker,** Management Guru and Author

Never have you had so many choices about how or when to communicate, not to mention how you're being bombarded with communication 24/7. With hybrid workplaces, communication is even more challenging. Cooperative communicators learn the preferred forms of communication of their colleagues. Cooperative communicators are sensitive and know when email communication isn't real-time enough. It's time to get on Slack, Facetime, text, call or charge into her office to have a face-to-face meeting.

What I like about video calls, face-to-face or even mobile calls is you can listen to the other person's tone of voice and so much more. In the case of video calls and face-to-face, you can also read people's body language, which is absent in email or any other form of digital written communication. You also get immediate

When people notice your active listening, they will respect you and open up to you.

feedback although you can get that with texting and Slack if the other person is responsive! But you still miss out on their tone of voice and/or body language.

Cooperative communicators are active listeners who listen with their eyes, ears and emotions. They observe body language, tune into the tone of voice, breathing, feelings and intention. "Cooperative communicators don't judge the person they're conversing with. They listen with an open mind.

Good listening will differentiate you from most people. Cooperative communicators are active listeners. When people notice your active listening, they will respect you and open up to you.

Incorporate the following cooperative intelligence practices and attitudes and you will benefit by building and maintaining professional relationships (Friendlies) that will be enduring.

- Treat your colleagues and clients with respect.

- Take a problem-solving attitude, but don't solve their problems.

- Identify helping opportunities with your contacts that are mutually beneficial.

- Be a source for acknowledgment and appreciation.

- Maintain a positive attitude.

- Don't take yourself too seriously.

- Promote continual communication.

Cooperative Intelligence Case Studies

I practiced cooperative intelligence as a telco CI Manager back in the 1980s although I hadn't named it yet. The sales force wanted a tactical comparison of our product features versus our key competitors' product features and pricing broken down by region. We outsourced this project and the sales force was very happy with the deliverable. If anything, we exceeded their expectations. I had recently come from Sales, so I wasn't guessing what they wanted. I knew what they needed.

Next, we produced software for Sales to price out competitive products versus ours. That was quite complex since we had to include our many tariffs. We then trained the sales force and sales support staff on how to use the software.

Sadly, one of our regions said they couldn't use the software, so we made changes to accommodate them and traveled to their location to train them. I brought along the software developer in case we needed to make more changes. I outsourced the training so I could attend the class to take notes and to observe how well it went.

During the first training session the key sales support person rudely interrupted the trainer to complain and insisted on some specific software changes. I noted them. We stayed up late and made the changes overnight. Early the next morning, the key sales support person called and said something very important had come up so was unable to attend the second training class. "Geez," I thought, "We stayed up half the night to make your changes, and you can't make the training session that you had previously committed to and insisted upon." I was so angry that some bad words flew out of my mouth, and I slammed down the phone. You could slam phones back then.

There were repercussions from this incident at high levels. But the upshot was that the salespeople appreciated how I had tried to support them and now fed me competitive information that was incredibly timely, including competitor product announcements well before they would be public. They were so excited to help me that they gave me competitive material that they shouldn't have, so I had to train them in ethics. I also found out this key sales support person was not liked by Sales, and somehow my angry incident gained me some respect. However, I don't recommend my bad behavior. I was in my early 30s and looked about 18, so often enough people didn't take me seriously.

The Science Behind Conversation

According to Organizational Anthropologist Judith Glaser, there is science behind conversation. In her book, *Conversational*

Intelligence: How Great Leaders Build Trust and Get Extraordinary Results, she writes about the "chemistry of conversations." Conversation triggers physical and emotional changes in the brain that either open a person to having a healthy, trusting conversation or close a person from fear or worry to speak carefully.

Managers' Positive and Negative Conversational Behaviors

They may be sending mixed messages.

Behaviors

Behavior	Frequency
Concern for others	Oxytocin-producing behavior
Truthful about what's on mind	
Stimulate discussion/curiosity	
Paint picture of mutual success	
Open to difficult conversations	
Don't trust others' intentions	Cortisol-producing behavior
Focused on convincing others	
Others are not understanding	
Pretend to be listening	
Emotions detract from listening	

0 Never   1   2   3   4   5 Always

Managers' Self-Reported Frequency

Source: Creating WE Institute/Qualtrics

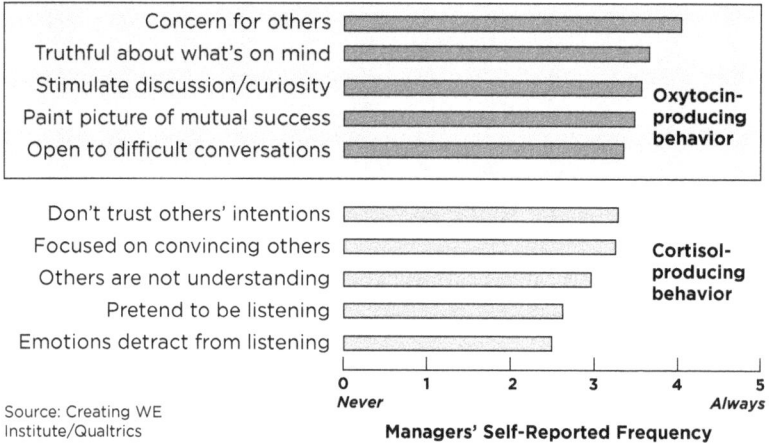

Behaviors that increase cortisol levels reduce "Conversational Intelligence" or "C-IQ," a person's ability to connect and think innovatively, empathetically, creatively and strategically with others. Behaviors that spark oxytocin raise "C-IQ." Sadly, oxytocin metabolizes more quickly than cortisol, so its effects are less dramatic and long-lasting.

Positive comments and conversations spur the production of oxytocin, a feel-good hormone that elevates your ability to communicate, cooperate and trust others by activating networks in your prefrontal cortex. When you express curiosity about her knowledge, stories, perspectives or successes, it releases dopamine.

When you are curious about him and ask questions, the heart connects to his brain, engaging him to open up. This sends a whole new path of neurotransmitters that enables you to connect with him.

When you face criticism, rejection or fear, your body produces a higher level of cortisol, which shuts down the thinking center of your brain. You become more reactive and sensitive and perceive greater judgment and negativity than actually exists. This can last 26 hours or more.

Glaser suggests six practices to promote win/win conversations that produce oxytocin, the feel-good hormone:

1. *Be open to influence.* Don't get addicted to being right.

2. *Prime yourself to trust.* Think about the good things that will happen.

3. *Be curious:* Ask questions for which you don't have answers.

4. *Listen* to discover what you don't know and to connect.

5. *Sustain conversation agility* that allows you to change in the moment.

6. *Rather than asking why,* look to understand where the other person is coming from by using words such as, "Help me understand …" or "What does success look like to you?"

In my experience, "why" is an aggressive and confrontational word.

When you come from your heart and speak the truth, people are going to feel it. "Research indicates that when we are comfortable with someone our heartbeat becomes more coherent, sending signals to the brain to open up, and share with that person." You will loosen their lips since she is not feeling defensive and judged. She will feel open and trusting.

Glaser reminds you that the words you use in conversations are rarely neutral. Words have histories informed by years of use. Each time a new experience overlays another meaning on a word, the information all gets collected in your brain to be activated during conversations. I also like to observe how he expresses himself: visually, by sound, feeling, etc., since I can adapt to that easily enough in conversation to make him more comfortable.

Refer to Chapter 15 for more detail under Verbal Expression: Yours and Theirs.

your turn

I challenge you to set a broad intention you'd like to use in business conversations.

You may have a different one, depending on the conversation.

Which cooperative intelligence practices and attitudes do you already use?

Which ones would you like to adopt?

How do you plan to adopt them?

Can you identify a role model to help you?

NEXT
Think of other cooperative intelligence practices.

If you're interested, read up on the science behind conversation. Sources are Glaser's book, videos and her company, The CreatingWE® Institute.

Observe how you feel when your cortisol levels rise—think stress, anger, frustration, angst. Notice how long it takes to release those feelings when your cortisol level rises.

Observe how you feel when your oxytocin levels rise (e.g., when you're listened to). Notice how long it takes for oxytocin levels to decline. It's not very long ... that's why you need to work on keeping the other person's oxytocin levels rising during a conversation.

**You create your thoughts,
your thoughts create your intentions,
and your intentions create your reality.**

—**Dr. Wayne Dyer,** American Self-Help Author and Lecturer

chapter ten

Pre-Execution: Motivation

People are naturally curious.

When conducting a conversation, it is helpful to know how people are motivated to share. Understanding human nature helps you encourage other people to want to share what they know.

Know Human Nature

Overall, there is a lack of listening ears. It's made worse by the hybrid workforce and digital communication that dominates these days. I predict that it will only get worse as AI in its many forms continues to develop.

While you can't read another person's mind, there are human tendencies that are simply human nature, which you want to be aware of when you're having a conversation.

People are naturally curious. As Dale Carnegie famously explains, the beauty of curiosity is that it makes you nearly irresistible to everyone around you. Curiosity makes people want to fill the gap between what they know and what they'd like to know. Your curiosity about them makes them want to talk.

People like to be recognized and appreciated. Everyone responds to this. For example, you might let her know you're interviewing her due to her industry expertise. Or you might point out something he or his company has done well.

People like to show off what they know. They want you to feel that they're well informed about their profession. They might share confidential information with fellow professionals such as lawyers or doctors. For example, there may be one upmanship between these professionals that gets them talking about their accomplishments.

People like to gossip. You need to know that most people can't keep a secret.

Many can't resist the urge to complain … some more than others. You can complain about something you want to hear more about.

People can't resist correcting others. In the same vein, people tend to prove someone else wrong. I notice most men can't resist the urge to correct me, a woman. Certain professions attract people who can't resist correcting others: teaching, advising, consulting, auditing, supervisors of all stripes and coaches. They underestimate the value of their knowledge, so share freely. Often, they question the other person's ability to understand it so they explain it even more thoroughly. Some people, professionally, just can't help themselves.

People can be defensive, especially if you're attacking or criticizing something they've said or produced. Or you attack something that another person said or wrote who they respect.

People tend to overtalk when emotional about something whether it's joy or sorrow. They can get caught up with a great accomplishment or success at work and be chatty about it. Or that their privately held company just had a major layoff of hundreds.

People can be modest about their accomplishments as well. They might downplay them in the "aw-shucks" mode and then tell you all about it.

Insecurity is a common human factor. This makes people feel inferior to others who they think are smarter or more educated than they are. This causes them to show others that they're as smart or smarter than they are. They are apt to correct you to cover up their insecurity.

Interviewer's Best Practices

Really big people are, above everything else, courteous, considerate and generous—not just to some people in some circumstances—but to everyone all the time.
—**Thomas J. Watson,** Founder of IBM

I find if I get into the present moment through one of those grounding exercises described earlier in Chapter 8, *Get Grounded*, I am most effective. Getting grounded makes me look forward to conversations. I am relaxed, yet focused and curious about what I might learn.

Here are a few skills of good conversationalists:

- *Natural gift for making friends* – Build a relationship with the other person.

- *Authenticity* – Be who you are. Don't act to manipulate the conversation.

- *Nonthreateningly curious* – Curious enough to listen to answers you weren't expecting and digging even deeper to learn more.

- *Broad general knowledge* – A generalist who can strike up a conversation about almost anything.

- *Good memory* – Not just overall but recalling a topic later in the conversation to gather more detail.

- *Two-level listener* – Listen for what's said and what's not said.

- *Appreciate cultural differences.* Welcome diversity in its many forms.

- *Empathy* – Try to understand what the other person is experiencing and are kind and gracious.

- *Politeness* – Express appreciation during the conversation and use words like "thank-you" and "please."

- *Spontaneity* – The ability to go with a changed flow of conversation. Find another path to get at what you'd like to learn and learn what you didn't know that you didn't know.

- *Flexibility* – Change communication style to the other person's without being manipulative.

- *Intuitive* – Take cues from how the other person is feeling and expressing to move the conversation along.

- *Discrete* – Give the other person confidence that you will not share points they'd like to remain just between you two.

Cue into How They're Motivated

When I interview a person, I wonder what will motivate him to share with me. One way is to consider the 5Ps and his Emotional Intelligence or EQ include:

1. **P**rofession

2. **P**olitics

3. **P**ersonal Issues

4. **P**ersonal Facts

5. **P**redisposition

1. Profession: People like that you appreciate the value of their profession. I like to learn:

- What do you do professionally?
- How long have you worked in this profession? Your company?
- Do you belong to a professional association? Which one(s)?
- What is your job title?
- How are you compensated for your work? Compensation can be other than money.
- Where have you worked previously?
- Where did you go to university? Or other specialized education?
- Do you have an advanced degree beyond a Bachelor's?

While people tend to be skeptical because of fake news and misinformation, they also tend to share more readily than they did before social media became common. As mentioned earlier, people working in certain professions are more apt to open up and so do disgruntled employees at any level. Factory workers often share whether blue collar or white collar. The challenge is getting to them since many factories run with few employees due to technical advances.

Technical people, whether it's software, hardware or those in the sciences, can be great informers. If you talk their talk and express appreciation for their profession, they will often open up. In some professions, it's best to hire someone who works in their industry since their knowledge is so specialized. That can be the case in technical fields such as AI, nanotechnology or medical fields like pharmaceuticals or medical devices.

Executives or those in professional occupations might test you and qualify you before they share such as doctors, accountants, financial analysts, contracts managers, lawyers or executives. However, I have learned that once I pass their test in conversation, they share quite readily.

2. Politics: I concentrate on learning more about their work politics since local, national and global politics have become too divisive. It's useful to be aware of people's politics so as not to unknowingly inflame them. I want to learn:

- What are you proud of?
- What is highly valued in your company's culture?
- What are the challenges that you face at your company?
- How do company politics affect your willingness to open up?
- What should I not talk about?
- What must I make sure to talk about?

3. Personal Issues: This includes relationships and habits outside of work, such as lifestyle, charitable causes, music, hobbies, passions, nature, sports they play and/or follow.

4. Personal Facts: This includes age, gender, sexual orientation, marital status, family situation, kids, pets, LGBTQ+ and religion. I also like to learn about their culture and where they grew up. We are so influenced by where and how we grew up. I am sensitive to that since I grew up in Japan and attended an international school. That has shaped my life and perspective in so many ways.

5. Predisposition: While a lot of people like the Myers-Briggs indicator of a person, I prefer D.i.S.C., but don't ignore the Myers–Briggs Type Indicator (MBTI). I particularly take note of a person's introversion or extroversion, two MBTI factors. If they are introverted you need to be extroverted to get them out of their shell. There is nothing like two introverts to kill a conversation, especially if you're pressed for time.

John Nolan, the king of elicitation, is highly introverted. Yet he was an excellent elicitation instructor. He said he required quiet time to regenerate after teaching class. But if you attended his class you would have thought he was an extrovert. He portrayed outgoing energy. If you're an introvert you can do this too. It just takes desire, persistence and practice.

Learning something about the 5Ps can give you insight into a person's behavioral style and motivation and provide an icebreaker for your conversation.

your turn

Have you noticed how people are motivated to share with you?

Which of the interviewer's best practices come naturally to you?

Which would you like to adopt?

Find a role model to advise you.

I challenge you to use the 5Ps to identify icebreakers for your next conversation.

> **You can make more friends in two months**
> **by becoming interested in other people**
> **than you can in two years by trying to get**
> **other people interested in you.**
>
> —**Dale Carnegie**

chapter eleven

Pre-Execution: Communication Style:
D.i.S.C. and EQ

Foreknowledge can help you to probe
more sensitively and effectively during your conversation.

I use D.i.S.C. to understand the behavior, fear and motivation
people exhibit as they communicate during our conversation.
According to Dr. Williams Marston, the creator of **D.i.S.C.** theory,
there are four personality types:

Dominant/Driver

Influencer/Socializer

Steady/Relater

Compliant/Conscientious/Thinker

If you understand how other people relate to you based on
your behavior style, you can modify your behavior to match theirs
more closely. The idea behind D.i.S.C. is to match or mirror the
communication style of the person you're talking with to make
her more comfortable. This is a balancing act since you want to be
authentic and not play act. At the same time, people often react
better when you're in synch with their D.i.S.C. behavior style.

D.i.S.C. Behavior Styles

Fast & Aggressive

Task Oriented ↓ / **People Oriented** →		
	Dominant/Driver: 18% **Motivation:** Bottom line results How much? How quick? Let's get going ... **Fear:** Losing control, wasting time **Behavior:** Self-assured, direct, forceful, impatient **Be:** Cut to the chase. Focus: results. Instant feedback	**Influencer/Socializer 28%** **Motivation:** Flattery, optimism, more emotional **Fear:** Rejection **Behavior:** Animated, talkative, open, charming, persuasive, Show emotions. **Be:** Give positive reinforcement. Smile. Make it fun. Tell story—> Emotion.
	Compliant/Conscientious/ Thinker: 14% **Motivation:** Accuracy and details **Fear:** Conflict, criticism, being wrong **Behavior:** Serious, analytical, observant. Questioning and skeptical. Cautious and reflective. Enjoys independence. **Be:** Expect many questions. Details, details, details. Supporting evidence. Silence works: let them think.	**Steady/Relater 40%** **Motivation:** Cooperative. Sincere. Need to like you to work with you. Others' needs first **Fear:** Change (not early adopters) **Behavior:** Careful, slow, calm, patient/relaxed, humble. Don't like to be rushed. Dependable. **Be:** Take a genuine iinterest in them. Map out each step. Be empathetic. Be likeable.

Steady & Cautious

Source: Adapted from Eric Barron's presentation, "Understand your clients better using the DiSC personality styles.

Dominant/Driver – are confident, driven and direct in their mannerisms. They are often risk takers and are more apt to cause an ulcer than to have one. The best way to communicate with this type is directly. Don't tell them stories and get right to the point. They are task oriented and motivated to achieve bottom line results. They fear losing control and wasting time. Their behavior tends to be impatient, self-assured and forceful.

Influencer/Socializer – are natural networkers and can be quite expressive in their communication. Focus on building a relationship as you communicate with an Influencer. If you're selling to an Influencer, supply testimonials and give them examples about who is using your product or service. They are more people oriented and tend to be animated, talkative, open, charming, yet also persuasive. They fear rejection and are motivated by optimism, flattery and are more emotional. Give them reinforcement and smile. Make it fun. Tell stories.

Steady/Relater – are people oriented, amicable and are uncomfortable with conflict. They are good listeners and collaborators who are loyal and sincere in relationships. They need to like you to work with you and place others' needs before their own. They don't like to be rushed and tend to be slow, calm, patient, relaxed and humble. Focus on the personal touch and make sure that you get back to them personally. Be likeable and empathetic and take a genuine interest in the Steady/Relater.

Compliant/Conscientious/Thinker – are often very bright, task-oriented and analytical. They are logical and detail-oriented and tend to micromanage. Be prepared for extensive questioning and provide details and supporting evidence in your answers. However, don't include your stories or small talk in your answers. They tend to be serious, observant, questioning, skeptical, cautious and reflective. They don't like to be wrong, criticized or in conflict. Like Dominants, they fear loss of control but also accuracy. Silence is appreciated by this type as it gives them time to think.

It's useful to notice which of these behavior styles are easiest for you to match. For example, I have an easier time matching with Influencer/Socializer and Steady/Relater behavior styles. I must adapt my behavior style the most with Dominant/Drivers but have learned with practice. The Compliant/Conscientious/Thinker is my biggest challenge since I am not a micromanager or that detail-oriented and can get impatient with all their questions.

No one person has exactly one of these four personality types. Predisposition is also affected by what is going on in a person's life. Emotions such as fear, stress or joy can change a person's normal predisposition, and that's why I like to consider a person's EQ.

How empathetic is the person you'll speak with? How do you think this will change under stress or other emotions? Empathy toward others often softens them. You're a fellow human being and you want to treat him as the individual he is.

The more you "know" her, the more you can sense how she might be feeling and thinking.

It's good to know a few things about the person you'll be speaking with so you can understand what her point of view might be. The more you "know" her, the more you can sense how she might be feeling and thinking. This foreknowledge can help you to probe more sensitively and effectively during your conversation. Even if you don't know the person beforehand, it's good to think how he might be so you can quickly adjust to his behavior style.

Sharing Dispositions

Over the years, I have observed the following eight sharing dispositions during conversations. You want to be observant of the other person and pick up on his general sharing disposition. It can also change during the conversation if you bring up something that excites him, makes him sad, is stressful or he has little knowledge about.

Sharing Disposition

Egocentric	Deeply Intelligent	Nerd	Helper
Motor Mouth	Intellectual	Clam	Evasive Deceptive

Egocentric – A know-it-all who doesn't know it all but wants you to think he knows it all. Don't waste your time but sometimes this person is good at referring you to someone else who is the subject matter expert you seek. Don't offend him in the process by asking him who else you should speak with or make him feel that he isn't good enough. Thank him for what he has shared, even though it wasn't what you were looking for. You want to leave people feeling good about themselves before you sign off.

Motor Mouth – These are the chatty ones who you must interrupt to stay on track. It can be a challenge to keep them on track since they are so talkative. Often enough they answer most of your questions without you asking and provide information that you didn't even know to ask about. During their flood of speech, I take notes on points I want to hear more about and interrupt them when I can.

Deeply Intelligent – These people know a lot and know the value of what they know: accountants, controllers, executives and lawyers. These folks are good targets since they can't resist the urge to correct you. But they might want to test you first to make sure you are credible and know what you're talking about. Once you gain their trust, these folks can be very helpful.

Intellectual – These people are knowledgeable like the Deeply Intelligent. But unlike the Deeply Intelligent, they don't realize the value of what they know. They are so steeped in their professional knowledge that they assume everyone else is too. They are proud of what they know and will share with little encouragement. Intellectuals are often teachers, technical experts, scientists and researchers. I've also encountered government workers who are intellectuals.

Intellectuals are extremely knowledgeable and happy to share. They also assume that you don't understand their profession and will go to great pains to explain things to you. They often expect that you'll have questions since you don't understand their profession or industry. I have had to train the technical experts I've worked with in the telco industry to restrain them from sharing, and to qualify those they would speak with before unleashing them at trade shows.

Nerd – These people are very intelligent in their space that is usually high tech. They tend to be programmers, software developers or app developers. Make sure you can talk their talk before you connect with them. If you can talk their talk, they are chatty about what they do. A great icebreaker is to express interest in learning more about their technical field. That has worked for me almost every time. Nerds are often introverted. I've noticed that once you get introverted nerds talking about something they're really interested in, they have a lot to say.

Clam – Many people can be a clam. You need to figure out why they're clams. Are they simply introverted and you need to draw them out? Are they having a bad day? Did they just receive sad news? Are they sick? Maybe you're catching them at a bad time. Maybe they struggle to express themselves. You'll need to gently prod them throughout the conversation. Be patient. Keep an open mind.

Sometimes a clam is happy to refer you to someone else who's knowledgeable that you wouldn't have found any other way.

Other times you need to reschedule your conversation or move on to someone else.

Helper – Many people want to be helpful. They can't resist answering your questions, sometimes falsely since they're trying to be helpful. They're embarrassed if they don't know what you're looking for so they make something up. I wish they'd let me know they don't know and refer me to someone else who does. But they usually don't. It's easy to identify this helper syndrome when you ask an in-depth question since they usually can't answer it confidently (if at all). You can observe this as their tone of voice might go flat or be uncertain and questioning. They'll often hesitate in their response to a more in-depth question since they don't know.

Evasive/Deceptive – If you suspect that a person is being evasive or deceptive, sometimes you just need to move on. But give him a chance before making a snap judgment. I'll usually test this person with a couple of questions that I know the answers to. Or I'll purposely state a fact that's wrong and see if he corrects me, and if so, how he corrects me.

your turn

Start observing the other person's preferred behavior style during your conversation.

Are there certain ones that are easier for you to match?

Which ones are harder for you to match?

Observe her sharing disposition.

Did her sharing disposition change at certain points during your conversation?

If so, how did it change? What do you think triggered the change?

**It is a narrow mind which cannot look
at a subject from various points of view.**

—**George Eliot,** English Victorian Novelist

chapter twelve

Pre-Execution:
Unique: Who Is She or He?

Self-awareness is a key to being a good conversationalist.

After this discussion about the 5Ps, D.i.S.C. and sharing dispositions, it can be too easy to pigeonhole the person you're speaking with into a persona box. Be aware of this. Remember every person you talk to is unique. Treat him as the individual he is and your conversation will flow. Observe and adapt to how she is behaving during the conversation and recognize when she changes.

- How do you sense uniqueness in another person?

- How does this come across as you converse with her?

- What can you do to be more sensitive to who he is, his individual needs and motivation?

Just before you have your conversation, review what you know about this person.

- Does something stand out that makes her unique?

- After considering the 5Ps, has your thinking changed about what her sharing disposition might be?

- What might she not want to share? Why? If it's important, how will you get her to share that specific piece of information you seek?

NPR's Fresh Air host Terry Gross matches the right line of questioning to the right subject. The best interviews are never one-size-fits-all. "There's no generic one question to me. It would depend on who the person is. I think one of the things about interviewing is that you don't ask the same thing of everyone. It would really depend. Is that person a painter? Is he an avant-garde jazz musician? Is he a politician, a priest? Who is she? Who is he?"

If you have spoken to this person before, review what he shared that might be relevant to your upcoming conversation. Maybe he shared something earlier that you didn't ask about but now you're curious to learn more about.

- What did he seem comfortable sharing?

- Why would he want to share more?

- Did anything you asked for or said make him appear or sound uncomfortable?

How Do You Come Across?

> Knowing others is intelligence;
> knowing yourself is true wisdom.
> —**Lao Tzu,** Chinese Philosopher

So far, I have concentrated on helping you learn how to know others. If you don't know yourself, how you come across naturally, and how people react to you, how can you adapt to how others communicate? How you come across matters more than wordsmithing exactly what you'll say. Knowing how you come across gives you the confidence and intelligence you need to adapt to the other person's communication style that opens him up to share with you. This also helps you to anticipate how he might answer. In the same vein, you don't want to take yourself too seriously since you need to be flexible and open. It's OK to dance a little bit verbally or with your visual expression to make him feel more comfortable.

How you come across matters more than wordsmithing exactly what you'll say.

Self-awareness is a key to being a good conversationalist. How do you do this? To learn more about how I come across, I have asked colleagues for their feedback and learned by reading attendee reviews of my presentations and workshops over the years. I have also listened to my recordings, especially Win/ Loss conversations, where I can't deny how I come across. Here is what I've discovered.

I am enthusiastic and have high energy. This is often infectious for getting people to open up. I have no problem being silent and listening. I was born curious (thanks, Mom) and love to listen to people's stories, which they sense almost immediately. I also love people (thanks, Dad). Whether talking to a stranger or to someone I am scheduled to interview, I often hear great stories without asking specific, probing questions. Many people have told me, "I haven't ever told anyone else this, but …."

I don't take myself too seriously. I am not a comedian, but I can take a joke and a smile comes easily. Yet, I can also be intense and persistent. I must guard against coming on too strongly on issues. Some people really like me while others don't. There does not seem to be a middle ground.

My voice sounds younger than my age. Whether I am speaking with a man or a woman (less often), I notice he or she often informs or corrects me even when I repeat the exact words back to either later in the conversation. This has also carried into video chats, where clearly I don't look young.

Here are a few words for how I come across when feedback is given: Positive, smiles easily, enthusiastic, authentic, cooperative, grounded, attentive, intentional, intense, persistent, curious, listens, chats, hates conflict.

Good Phrases to Use Based on Who You Are
I've learned what phrases work to promote sharing regardless of the other person's apparent communication preference/D.i.S.C. It's a balancing act to figure this out. It's a combination of who I am, how I come across, and how I notice people respond to me. It took me years to make a note of these phrases, and it changes over time, as speech changes. I remember when people started to say, "No worries" or "It looks chill."

Here is a sample of the phrases that encourage others to share with me. I challenge you to come up with your own list!

- Thank you for taking the time for our conversation.

- I wonder if you might be able to help me ….

- This call is about you … and your experience with ….

- Nobody seems to know ….

- Wow, that is really helpful ….

- Great!

- Really … that's interesting ….

- Really!?

- I'm curious ….

- I'm confused ….

- Can you help me understand …?

- Is this what you mean? (clarification)

- Thank you for your feedback, this has been so helpful ….

- I'm sorry to hear that. What would make it better?

- How can we improve …?

- I've covered what I had in mind, but is there something important to you that we haven't discussed?

- I think we've covered everything, but there is one last thing I wonder about ….

- Hmm. (listening)

- I see. (listening)

- I hear you. (listening)

- I understand. (listening)

- Oh sure. (agreeing)

There are three practices that work well for me to promote sharing:

- Quote relevant reported facts that I've heard or read somewhere.

- Paraphrase or repeat words the other person has said.

- Match body language including the other person's breathing.

Adrian Alvarez, CEO of Midas Consulting based in Argentina, has his new people spend time getting comfortable with their own style. You need to be true to yourself. You need to be comfortable with how you are before you can effectively interview others. If you fake it, it shows.

For example, in some languages like Spanish and French, people use the more formal version for the word *you* while others will take the more familiar version for the word *you*. If you're comfortable with you and your style, it's much easier to hold conversations, and people will be more responsive since they sense you're authentic and comfortable in your own skin.

your turn

Take a personal inventory.

• What is your predisposition around conversation?

• Are you comfortable in conversation? Why or why not?

• Do you enjoy conversation? Why or why not?

• Are you naturally curious?

• How do you feel about people? Do you enjoy people?

• What are the strengths you bring to a conversation?

• What gets in the way of a flowing conversation?

• Do you know how you come across to those you speak with? Elaborate on this.

After you've answered these questions, ask some colleagues about how you come across since it's easy to be blindsided. Maybe they would like to answer some of the above questions about you.

The human being is single, unique, and unrepeatable.

—Pope John Paul II

chapter thirteen

Execute:
Execute the Call

Learn and respect the culture you're dealing with.

Before we get into the details of executing the call, let's identify some rules of engagement for conversation.

Be polite and respectful. If you are polite to the people you speak with, they will take you more seriously and are usually more responsive.

Be prompt for your call or meeting. Greet the person warmly and with enthusiasm. Let her know how grateful you are that she took the time to have this conversation with you.

Respect their time and expertise. I work hard to hold my conversations to the agreed upon time. However, I struggle with this when the other person is on a roll that takes us past our time. She is enjoying our conversation and sharing valuable information. I also hate to interrupt her since it seems rude. This is a balancing act, and you need to be sensitive to the other person to call it right.

Listen with an open mind and ask reflective questions.

Respect their culture. In the US direct eye contact is important, even on video calls. In other cultures, it can be offensive. In many Western cultures you shake hands to greet each other. In Japan, you bow. Learn and respect the culture you're dealing with.

Speak slowly so they understand you, especially if they don't speak your language fluently. Checkpoint more often to make sure they understand you and you understand them.

Use proper grammar and stay away from too much slang, especially if the other person doesn't speak your language fluently.

Be sensitive to those who are hard of hearing. If you can see the person, you'll notice he's reading your lips and his eyes are more strained than someone who hears well.

Don't pretend to hear. Ask him to repeat if you didn't hear something that you think is important.

Don't interrupt or finish her sentence. Use words that express appreciation and good manners, like please and thank you but not obsequiously.

Don't be accusative even if you feel it was "his fault."

Now, it's time to have that conversation! But wait, you still need to contact the person you want to speak with.

Get to the Right Person
Financial Incentives or Not
Consider if you need to provide a financial incentive in return for someone's time. This depends on the type of research you're doing, the industry you're working in and the company culture.

For example, in the medical profession, doctors expect monetary remuneration for their time. Others will only give you information if you give them something in return, such as a summary of your findings. You need to make sure that the summary doesn't contain anything proprietary but gives the person something valuable.

I'm of a mixed mind about providing financial incentives. In some cases, when I've offered monetary remuneration, I feel the person agreed to have a conversation with me for the money and the conversation was not fruitful. Another form of remuneration is to donate to a charity. This is more popular in my experience than providing a gift card. Sometimes, I give people the choice to receive a gift card or a donation to a favorite charity.

In other cases, I feel the person I am targeting is almost insulted if I offer to pay her to have a conversation. She is grateful that I am reaching out to have a conversation with her. This is an opportunity to share things with me about her experience with the company who has hired me that she might not be comfortable sharing with that company directly.

There are some instances where you cannot offer financial compensation: any type of US government employee and most European countries. In some European countries you can offer to give a donation on their behalf to a charity of their choice. It also depends on the practices of the company they work for.

Factor in Enough Time to Connect

Make sure you factor in the time it takes to get to the right person(s) for your conversation. Let's assume you have found the right people to talk to. Now you must get them to agree to have a conversation with you. Many forget about this step of connection and under-

estimate how long it takes to connect. Once you get to the right
person, you need to get on her calendar for your conversation.

My first choice is to have someone introduce me to the
other person. Most of my work is customer conversations with a
company's largest customers, so the Account Executive makes the
introduction. It might take several tries to get them to agree to a
call. Even with the Account Executive's

**These days, most of
my conversations are
held via video chats.**

intro, not all customers agree to have
a conversation. If they do, it might be
three weeks or as long as six weeks out.
In other cases, a company employee from another area of the
company makes the introduction. I used to make cold calls, but
with caller ID and all the robocalling, few people answer their
phone unless you're in their e-directory or they're expecting your
call.

These days, most of my conversations are held via video
chats. So, I don't need to know the other person's phone number.
I simply let him pick a good time by looking at my e-calendar.
If I'm asked to specify a few good times, I assume they don't like
e-calendar scheduling technology. If she has a last-minute schedule
change and can't make the video call, I give her the option to have
our conversation via mobile. Most prefer a mobile phone call
over another video call. Sometimes I text rather than email to get
connected if I find out that's her preferred way to communicate.
If I've emailed her several times and she hasn't responded, I will
send a short text in hopes of getting connected. As you can see,
you need to be persistent to schedule conversations.

Sometimes, I will call into an office to get through to the
person, if I don't have a referral and I don't have his email. Or

I'll call the office after I have emailed this person and he's been unresponsive. Sometimes, I find out he's left the company or she is away on maternity leave.

The point is you're dealing with another human being, so you need to be flexible and creative. When you call him when he is unresponsive to your email introduction, you can blame technology. Sometimes your email doesn't pass through his company's firewall. In my experience people feel bad when they realize my email didn't get through their company firewall, especially when I tell them I've tried three or four times. On those occasions, some will give me time right on the spot. You need to be prepared for that. One time I wasn't, but my mobile connection was so bad that I offered to call right back on my landline. Phew, I could grab my questions.

> **You're dealing with another human being, so you need to be flexible and creative.**

Getting Past Admins

When you get the gatekeeper, act as though you have a right to speak with the boss. I simply ask to speak with the boss in a confident way, not volunteering why unless I'm asked. But I'm ready if asked. For example, "I'm told she is the only person who knows about this. Can you help me?"

Another tactic is to ask the admin for the best time to call back. Sometimes the admin gives you the name of a better person to speak with once you say what you're looking for. These days he'll transfer you to that person. Just make sure you get the person's full name so you can ask for him by name if you need to call him later or get disconnected. With the correct name you can use an automated switchboard to connect.

Sometimes you need to be creative to work your way around admins. They go to lunch, hopefully not at the same time as the executive you're trying to reach. A colleague told me the story of her most creative executive connection. She couldn't get past the executive's admin. She had left several messages with the admin to no avail. In frustration, she had the admin paged to the company's main reception desk a few floors below the admin's office. My colleague immediately hung up and called the executive and had a great conversation.

I accidentally misdialed some years ago and the person who answered transferred me to the right person. So, sometimes in desperation, I'll dial a number just a little off from the main number and apologize when the "wrong" person answers. I'll explain who I'm looking for (if I have a name) or that I'm looking for an expert in X. That's another way to get transferred to where you need to be. Plus, you can tell the targeted person that a fellow employee (name) recommended that you talk with her. The call just got friendlier.

your turn

What are some of the tactics you have used to connect with the person you want to talk with?

Have a discussion with your colleagues and learn some other tactics.

Try them out.

**All truths are easy to understand
once they are discovered:
The point is to discover them.**
—Galileo Galilei

chapter fourteen

Execute: Build Rapport

If the person is active on social media,
you can learn a lot before you talk to him.

Building rapport is something you want to do as quickly as you can in your limited time for the conversation. It's words, tone, confidence, expression and how you make the other person feel that count, and you want to build trust.

You want to have the steps from Planning and a few more in mind as you start your conversation.

- Build off your Introduction and the 5Ps. (Planning/ Pre-Execution)

- Observe them visually. (video or in-person)

- Observe their speech, accent, speed, tone and breathing.

- Try to establish a quick, personal connection.

- Observe their communication disposition. (D.i.S.C.)

- Are they introverted or extroverted?

- What's their sharing disposition?

- Adapt your communication style accordingly, but don't fake it.

• Share but don't dominate. (unless that's your style and it works)

Make a Good First Impression

Smile. People can feel your smile even if you're not on their screen. As Dolly Parton says, "If you see someone without a smile, give them yours."

Give them your undivided attention. Theodore Roosevelt said, "People don't care how much you know, until they know how much you care." People can feel when you're in a hurry or are not being attentive. You might think you're a great multitasker, but people can tell when you're multitasking on a call and it hurts.

Give them your listening ears. As Stephen Covey famously said, "Most people do not listen with the intent to understand; they listen with the intent to reply." Ask yourself what's important to him and how you can add value.

Make the other person feel respected for who he is, and what he does. When building rapport, it helps to think about the person you're interacting with and to tailor your speech at least somewhat to him. You don't want to overcompensate the way people sometimes do when speaking with a child or being obsequious. That will only insult or confuse him.

People can feel your smile even if you're not on their screen.

Consider the other person's needs as you speak intending to make him more comfortable.

Here are some common icebreakers to get you started with your conversation.

- I read your article on …. It was excellent. I wonder about ….

- Thanks for agreeing to have a conversation. Is this still a good time? (especially if you feel her anxiety, sense shallow breathing or a stressful expression)

- Comments on the weather or "How's your weather?"

- Sports if they're enthusiasts.

- You seem so familiar. Where have we met? (Mention where it might have been.)

- I hear you're the best ….

- I heard that ….

- I see that ….

- Industry experts say ….

- Can you help me?

- So, what is it you do at company X?

- Something you have in common: "Oh, I see you have a cat, so do I." (school, locale, pets, hobbies, sports, culture, travel experiences)

- You won't believe the day I'm having (emotional tug), especially if you already know the person.

Building Rapport: John Thomson's Experience

One of my favorite stories about building rapport is John Thomson's story. He is the Chief Research Officer and Director of Field Intelligence at Aurora WDC, a strategic and competitive intelligence consulting firm. In years past, John worked in collection, particularly

HUMINT (human intelligence). HUMINT is getting another person to share what you are looking for during a conversation. Yes, he's an expert at loosening lips!

The Situation

This was a very difficult project. John was working for a client in the tech industry. They were studying a small startup tech company. This company had announced that it was introducing a new technology platform that was going to be highly disruptive. John's client was very nervous when they saw this announcement, which was just a vague press release. They wanted to know as many details as possible about the platform.

They engaged Aurora WDC to find the details. As this was a very small tech company, John knew he probably had just one shot with such a limited resource pool. He started with the source process: identify the company employees who likely had access to the information that his client was seeking.

John's Approach: Planning

John researches every source that he identifies to find out as much about them as possible. It's much easier these days with social media. In doing this research, John tries to find information to determine a few things to build rapport with the person he'll be interviewing.

Might there be a common interest or share something in common that he can leverage to build rapport with that person and make him feel comfortable talking with him? John looks for the person's hobbies, interests, where he grew up, where he went to school, if he has a pet and if so, what kind.

He asserts, "It has to be genuine though! You can't just make something up." For example, "I see you love NASCAR." The other person says, "So do I." You risk that the other person will want to talk about NASCAR and you really can't. You had better be able to back up the statements you make.

John also uses source research to gauge the person's personality.

- Does he seem more introverted or extroverted?

- Is he highly opinionated?

- Does he have conflict issues?

If the person is active on social media, you can learn a lot before you talk to him.

John also tries to assess what might motivate the other person to talk. Is there anything he can leverage? Often, it's ego, ideology, or money. For example, John might see that he wrote a white paper, presented at a conference, or was quoted in a news article. These are great ways to stroke his ego and make him feel good about himself.

Pre-Execution

In this project, John hit the jackpot! He identified the Senior Product Manager at this startup tech company, whom we'll call Bill. John knew Bill was likely to have all the answers to his client's questions. When he checked Bill's LinkedIn bio, he saw that Bill had attended the Berklee College of Music in Boston and had studied guitar before taking a career shift into technology.

To better understand this, outside of work semi-professional guitarists have a passion for music. John is a semi-professional guitarist. Musicians tend to share a common bond with each other that's almost metaphysical. When they meet each other for the first time and learn about each other's musical passion, nine times out of ten, they make friends with each other. John decided to use music as his door opener to build rapport with Bill.

Execution of the Interview
John opened the call by letting Bill know he'd looked at his LinkedIn profile. John said, "I have a very important question for you. Speaking as a fellow guitarist, I just have to know what it was like to attend the Berklee College of Music?" Bill laughed and they chatted about guitars and equipment for almost ten minutes. This is often not recommended during the brief time you have allocated for such a conversation. But John knew this was his only opportunity to get this information, so he needed to make Bill feel comfortable.

Consider an icebreaker or icebreakers that will work before each conversation you have.

John could tell that Bill was enjoying the conversation and so was he. Finally, Bill asked, "How can I help you?" They immediately launched into the discussion about Bill's company. John collected everything that his client wanted to know. Bill gave him more time on the call than John had originally asked for. This call was successful and it came from spending time developing rapport to make Bill feel comfortable with John as a fellow semi-professional guitarist!

your turn

Create a list of icebreakers that you are comfortable using.

Ask your colleagues for some that they use.

Now, consider an icebreaker or icebreakers that will work before each conversation you have.

Happy connecting!

**You don't get a second chance
to make a good first impression.**

Old Saying

chapter fifteen

Execute: Observe Verbal and Nonverbal Communication for Cues

When trying to read micro expressions, focus on the person's face, especially the eyes, eyebrows and mouth.

Judge the emotional state of the person you're speaking with:

• Is this the right time to ask or comment?

• Will what I say or my visual expression make him anxious or squirm?

Visual Cues

With the increasing use of video calls, you can read more of the body, at least the head, neck, shoulders and hands if she uses them. Visual cues are often a good indication of a person's emotional state.

Be aware of intentional body actions. When you are on a video call, think about what's visible: facial expressions and hand-to-face gestures. One common one is a smile when she doesn't mean it, and her eyes aren't smiling but might be glaring. The words don't complement a true smile. This is referred to as leakage: when the body expression and the spoken words don't match up. When I see a phony smile and hear words that go with it but see glaring eyes, I am skeptical. I believe the glaring eyes. She is angry about something.

Micro Facial Expressions

JP Ratajczak, Competitive Intelligence Director at Nationwide, shared the following tip in Jonathan Calof's book, *Gaining Market Insight from Events.* "People have a microsecond-long reaction to situations before they can mask their feelings." This is before the brain checks the expressed emotion. Thus, micro expressions disclose the true feelings someone is experiencing in that moment. Micro expressions can be hard to detect as that's just 1/25th of a second, according to micro expression expert Dr. Paul Ekman.

When trying to read micro expressions, focus on the person's face, especially the eyes, eyebrows and mouth. You can see them easily on video calls. Seven micro expressions are generic to everyone: fear, anger, disgust, surprise, contempt, happiness and sadness.

Micro Expressions

Fear	Raised eyebrows, tensed eyelids, lips stretched horizontally
Anger	Lowered eyebrows, tensed eyelids, lips pressed together
Disgust	Lowered eyebrows, wrinkled nose, raised upper lip
Surprise	Raised eyebrows, widened eyes, open mouth
Contempt	Narrowed eye on one side, corner of mouth rasied on same side
Happiness	Crow's feet around both eyes, raised cheeks, smile on lips
Sadness	Lowered eyebrows, drooping eyelids, downturned mouth

Note: context is critical when interpreting micro expressions. Consider the situation and the person's other body language, tone of voice and words to better understand her feelings. A great resource to study micro expressions is Dr. Paul Ekman's site *www.PaulEkman.com*. Do a search for "micro-expressions." Dr. Ekman has written numerous books and articles on reading emotions and deception through expressions.

Involuntary Body Actions

Beware when visual cues change markedly or even subtly during your conversation. Examples are: person starts to frown; looks at you questioningly; squirms in his chair; changes posture; cracks his knuckles. Or she suddenly starts tapping her feet, which is not her normal nervous habit. When you notice these changes, you might wonder if you've gone too long in a conversation, if you're probing about something that makes him uncomfortable or he doesn't know about. Observe that anxious people may also blink rapidly or close their eyes for a long time. When people wrinkle their lips, they may not agree with what you're saying.

JP Ratajczak also shares, "Showing the tongue, even just the tip, is usually an unconscious sign of disagreement. When people are about to say something they don't really want to say or are uncomfortable saying, they tend to cover their mouths."

Involuntary body actions to look for that often indicate discomfort include:

- Pupil Dilation: Alarm, Excitement, Interest, Satisfaction
- Jutting Jaw
- Speed Breathing
- Loss of Eye Contact
- Change of Posture: Leaning Away from You
- Twisting and Intertwining Hands

- Crossing and Uncrossing Legs

- Hand Pushing Hair Back

Since most of this body action is involuntary, it gives clues as to the validity of the response.

One of my favorite stories about involuntary body action comes from the Hollywood Squares TV show. The movie stars look so calm, collected and grounded. You see them only from the waist up. The tables are draped with tablecloths that hide the bottom half of their bodies, the land of involuntary body action. In one program, the producer lifted the draped tablecloths unbeknownst to the movie stars, so you could see lower body action. Their feet were tapping, toes curling, ankles entwining.

In general, it's the shoulders, arms, hands, legs, feet and general body posture where leakage is more apt to occur if it's involuntary body action. Aside from shoulders, you don't see these during video calls unless you have a full view of the person.

In Western cultures, you need to share eye contact with someone around 60-70% of the time to build good rapport.

One of my favorite, timeless books to learn how to read the body is *What Every BODY Is Saying: An Ex-FBI Agent's Guide to Speed-Reading People* by Joe Navarro with Marvin Karlins, PhD.

Reading Eyes

I've always been observant of a person's eyes. My husband has the most beautiful, engaging, and expressive blue eyes. It's one of the reasons I married him over 40 years ago.

"The eyes are the window to the soul," is an ancient saying supported by many scientific studies linking pupil dilation and eye gaze to mental states such as attention and intention. I believe eye contact is a powerful link to human connection.

Since most conversations are via video chats these days, it's worth observing the other person's eyes and how the eyes change during a conversation. In Western cultures, you need to share eye contact with someone around 60-70% of the time to build good rapport.

People often look up when they're ready for the conversation to end.

The direction that one looks can suggest a person's thought processes, including how engaged she is, whether she's telling the truth and how she feels about her conversation partner.

Looking to the left – Glancing to the left suggests that a person is trying to remember something or is having visual thoughts. I do this often when I'm trying to remember people's names, which I struggle with. This can also mean that someone is having a conversation with himself or is thinking about what he'll say next.

Looking to the right – Typically, looking to the right signifies lying. You tend to look to the right when you are imagining things, and towards the left when you are remembering. However, it is thought that looking to the right and downward suggests self-doubt, while looking to the right and up indicates lying.

Looking up – Glancing upward usually suggests that a person is bored or impatient with your conversation. People often look up when they're ready for the conversation to end.

Looking down – When a person looks downward when speaking to someone he views as more powerful, it can be a sign of submission or shyness. Or it might indicate that he is nervous or hesitant about taking part in the conversation. Or he may be processing a feeling.

When a person looks away during the conversation, she is often thinking and trying to get clarity of her thoughts. When looking directly at the other person, this may indicate that you like her, are interested in her, or want to threaten her. So, you need to rely on other facial displays and/or verbal communication to determine what those gazing eyes indicate.

Rapid eye blinking can indicate stress. A person's blink rate increases when troubled, aroused, nervous, or concerned, but returns to normal when he is relaxed.

Sometimes a person will make little to no eye contact when he's lying. However, the opposite can also be true. He might try to overcompensate when speaking to you by making too much eye contact. In some cultures, little eye contact is normal.

Impatience and Lack of Engagement

Knowing how to show impatience or urgency encourages the other person to be efficient. For example, when you look away or at your watch, an extrovert might talk even more to get you to pay more attention to him. But don't get too carried away showing your impatience. If he feels too hurried it may be distracting, and he might not be able to think and express himself clearly.

Just imagine how much more you can keep your conversation on track by being more visually observant.

As with all communication, you need to be looking for the following signals from the other person. These impatient gestures can be a cue that it's time to change the subject and re-engage with him. In other cases, it's time to wind up the conversation. He is done!

- Cracking of knuckles registers impatience and perhaps that the other person is nervous. This is the time to change the subject and get back on track.

- When you see or hear the tapping of a foot, it often indicates impatience, but it can also be a nervous habit.

- Going to folded arms can mean she is trying to really concentrate; or with an impatient facial expression, this can mean she's had enough.

- When he leans forward as if he's going to stand up, that's impatience at work.

- When he looks at his watch, it's a sign that it's time to wrap it up.

- When his voice becomes dull, he's become less engaged.

- When she yawns, it usually means she's tired or bored.

- Lean forward: When a person supports his face with a hand on a bent elbow, he is tired and not so engaged.

- A look of disbelief can be more effective than words with just about anyone. Like a picture tells 1,000 words, so does a visual expression.

You can make these impatient gestures or notice the other person is for any of these actions. Remember, visual observation goes both ways. I've noticed that most visual eye expressions are instinctive. Just imagine how much more you can keep your conversation on track by being more visually observant.

Verbal Cues

Be patient and stay alert. Maintain good posture even if you're not on video. Listen for the right cues to ask your questions or to make comments even if it's just to agree or say, "Hmm" or "Uh huh."

Here are the mostly auditory cues I look for as I listen and converse. It's mostly how they change as we talk. You're gauging where to go next with every sentence, so you need to listen carefully for these cues.

- Voice change: tone, loud, soft, faster, slower, brief silence

- Breath change: shallow, deep, a sigh, gasping, yawning, sniffling, coughing

- Expressiveness: change in sharing disposition, engagement, excitement, sadness, anxiety, silence

- Feeling: Intuitive space. Something is different or changing. Hard to express, but you notice it.

Tone changes usually indicate a different level of knowledge or engagement. When she can't see you, it's even more important to choose your words carefully. It's also important to have a tone that is trustworthy and confident, yet friendly. Notice his breathing pattern. If it changes, what seems to have triggered it? One way to make the person more comfortable is to mirror his breathing. This comes naturally as you become more observant and practiced. This is part of listening, not just the words but all the signals you observe from the other person.

Listening and Intuition: Case Study

I had an interesting experience where intuition was my driver. This was a cold call in the electrical measurement meter project. I had conducted 20 conversations by the time I got to this one. When the gentleman answered the phone, I noticed there was no background noise compared to the others who I had spoken with. So I asked him, "Where are you?"

He answered, "I'm in my crane."

Oh, I thought, *How quickly can I get him off the phone and figure out a better time to speak with him?* I told him I couldn't believe that he answered his phone while operating a crane. I chewed him out and asked if we could talk when he was safely on the ground. We spoke at lunchtime that day and he was most informative. I had gotten his attention by asking where he was. Obviously I had no way of knowing since I couldn't see him. I just sensed something was different. That's how intuition can work.

Bob Berkman, Information Professional, Editor and Media Studies Professor, provided a great definition of intuition. "Intuition works best when it's informed. It is … our ability to tap into the knowledge that we have acquired over time but cannot articulate consciously."

Two-Level Listening

Be a two-level listener for what he says and what you feel he left out that you thought he would know and would want to talk about. Learn to adapt your questions when the other person isn't who you thought she'd be.

Case Study: Two-Level Listening

Here is another story about interviewing users of meters that measure electrical current. All the questions we wanted answered were geared towards the user's experience with these instruments. I had talked to about 30 meter users by the time I reached this individual and could almost ask the questions in my sleep.

He answered his phone and said he'd be happy to tell me about using this handheld electronic technology. I asked which models he used. He said, "Actually I repair these handhelds."

I threw my questions aside and asked him which ones he repaired the most often and what he thought about the quality of the market leader's handheld. He seldom needed to repair the market leader's product due to its superior quality. He went on and on about the market leader's high-quality product compared to all the competition. He gave me some specific information about each of the major competitor's handhelds. All the competitors' meters were the same heavy, clunky product. They weighed a lot more than the market leader's product and were of inferior quality.

I also asked him what he thought about the state of the marketplace, how it had changed in the last 10 years and where he saw it going. This was key information my client wanted to learn. The individual users didn't have as much insight into these issues. This calibration professional was the most knowledgeable person I interviewed for the project. If I had stuck with the questions the client and I had agreed upon, it would have been a missed opportunity.

Verbal Expression: Yours and Theirs

Remember the value of using the right words. Don't be careless. Use words that promote sharing. Use "I" rather than "we" when you are speaking your mind. Don't be negative by using words like never or shouldn't. Don't show your opinion by using "always." You want to hear what they're thinking rather than influencing them with your bias. Don't use too much slang but use industry jargon as appropriate to build your credibility.

Remember that people are more comfortable relating if you use language that engages their senses. You can tell which sense they favor or relate to by listening to how they express themselves.

Visual people are interested in how things look or will look. They often focus on the future and have a big picture, strategic focus. Visual speakers might use colors or visual descriptions as they talk to you. Use visual words to express yourself in the conversation if you can. Words/phrases to use: see, look, appear, show, dawn, view. "I can picture what you're saying. I don't see it the same way. I can see what you mean. How does this look to you? It's unclear."

I am more auditory, and less visual than most. I must be on the lookout since many people I speak with are more visual and are quicker than me. Like most auditory people, I am easily distracted by noise and live in the moment. Tone of voice is important to me. Words/phrases to use: hear, listen, sound, harmonize, music. "I hear you. That rings a bell. How does this sound? Clear as a bell. Listen to this. Did you hear that …?"

Others are more emotional. They need more extensive detail to process information and respond to touch. Words/phrases to use: feel, touch, grasp, get a hold of, slip through. "Does it feel right? Do you grasp this idea? This doesn't feel right to me. This makes me feel uncomfortable. That must have made you feel so good." Feeling words often work with people who are intuitive.

Some people respond better to more logical and analytical phrases. They like detail, structure and order. Words/phrases to use: think, learn, process, understand. "

So, does this make sense to you?

This is a great way to learn.

Do you think this is a good idea?

Did I understand you correctly?

I'm not sure I follow your logic.

In reality, people jump among these communication preferences depending on what you're talking about. Sometimes you
can't detect a communication style quickly enough during a short
business conversation. So, pepper words of each of the communication preferences, and note what they seem to resonate with
most by observing their expression and listening to their tone of
voice and words.

Going Off-Topic
Sometimes I go off-topic intentionally or it happens unintentionally
in the middle of a conversation. It's often one of my cats passing
in front of the video camera that triggers this. I know many dog
lovers tell me this happens when their dog starts barking during
a conversation. Usually this has the effect of making the other
person more relaxed unless they're dominant and task-oriented.
Then they are more likely to view this as an unwelcome interruption.

Watch your time. Don't spend too much time off-topic. The
clock is ticking and time is precious. That said, I have gotten to
a different place in a conversation when this has happened with
more people-oriented individuals. (Influencers, Steady/Amicable)

I was speaking on one of my own *loss calls* with a lady who
had just come back from maternity leave. She chose a competing
service provider. This call was more delicate since my client had
been the incumbent for the business. Initially, the former customer
used her maternity leave as an excuse not to tell me the bad news
about why her company had not selected my client's software. My
client's salesperson had only reached out to her company close to
the time for contract renewal, a problem I hear too often.

We had our conversation, and I mentioned something in
the end about her baby, thinking we were done. Suddenly, she just

opened up and told me the key reasons why they had selected another service provider. "We had never been treated like a customer or partner and had to figure out how to use the software on our own. What we were looking for was a partnership with the company." My client's company had not provided it. This was particularly disappointing.

your turn

Observe visual cues in your next conversation.

Study Paul Ekman's facial micro expressions. Start noticing them during your conversations. It takes a lot of practice!

Listen for the verbal cues from this chapter. (Voice, Breath, Expression, Feeling)

How does that person express himself as the conversation flows? Visual, Auditory, Feeling, Analytical?

Now, try using words that correspond with how he expresses himself. (Visual, Auditory, Feeling, Analytical)

How did that work for you? How did the conversation flow?

Try going off-topic briefly and see where it takes you. When you came back to your planned conversation, how did it go?

Now combine what you see, hear and feel (intuition). What do you notice that you might have missed previously?

**Language matters.
It's the raw material of a story,
it changes how we feel about ourselves
and others, and it's a portal to connection.**
—**Brené Brown,** *Atlas of the Heart*

chapter sixteen

Execute:
Be Flexible

Don't get attached
to your preconceived assumptions.

I can't emphasize enough the need to be flexible. You need
to prepare for potential contingencies during your conversation.
Conversations often don't go as planned, even if you are thoroughly
prepared. That's when you need to be spontaneous and not take
yourself too seriously. I had to deal with an ethical situation in
Chapter 7, *Plan: Prepare Your Introduction and Ethics*. Here is the
rest of the story on how flexibility was my asset at a trade show.

It was my first Neocon, the largest North America-based
commercial interior and design trade show. I was asked to get
specific information on three competitors. I had done my homework before the conference. I knew where the competitors' exhibits
were in the huge Chicago Merchandise Mart. I had memorized
considerable facts about each competitor and had my client's
questions organized in my mind. I was sure of my game plan.

I went to the market leader's exhibit area and asked to have
a tour of their showroom, which featured some new products.
A snooty salesperson asked if I had an appointment. "Why no," I

stammered. "I didn't know I needed an appointment just to see your furniture display." So, I walked away feeling dejected. To add spice to the day, I was rapidly losing my voice.

What was I to do? I could not succeed in my assignment unless I could get into the competitor's showroom and get answers to my client's questions. I also needed to get in there soon before I lost my voice! Then, I got an idea: "Why couldn't I find a group who had an appointment and just tag along?" I stood outside the market leader's showroom, just out of sight, until I saw a group of gentlemen from a well-known software firm heading to this competitor's exhibit. I asked if they had an appointment and when they answered in the affirmative, I asked if I could tag along. "Sure," they said. "Happy to have you join us."

Ironically, the snooty salesperson was their account rep who gave us the tour and was as informative as she could be. She told us all about their new products and why they were better than the competition, which answered most of my client's questions. She glared at me, but graciously answered my questions, since I imagine this was one of her largest accounts.

Conversations often don't go as planned, even if you are thoroughly prepared.

This software firm was expanding exponentially. Meanwhile her software clients had questions that I hadn't thought of, as they were steeped in the commercial office furniture industry. Their work positions varied among purchasing, design and decision-making, so you can just imagine how much I learned. All because I was flexible and thought to hang back and wait for a customer and join their tour. I was also lucky that this was such a major customer!

Be Aware of Your Assumptions

Your assumptions about the other person may be wrong such as their state of mind, what motivates them, how they like to communicate or how you expect they'll respond to you. Don't get attached to your preconceived assumptions. You need to be open to recognize when your assumptions are wrong and flexible enough to change gears.

Assumptions Case Study: Lessons Learned

I had this experience in a project where I was trying to help a client in the glass business figure out how much longer a competitor would stay in this business. The competitor was mostly in unrelated businesses and wasn't focused on the glass business. They were losing money in glass and investing very little in it.

This competitor was publicly held and my client suggested that I listen to the competitor's quarterly earnings call. I replied, "I'll just read the report later." "No," he insisted, "I want you **to listen** to the earnings call." Inwardly I thought, *What a waste of time. You never learn anything in those overly rehearsed earnings calls.* But I reluctantly answered, "Yes, OK, I'll do it."

The earnings call was its usual overly rehearsed event until one analyst asked, "And how about the glass business?" The CEO's tone of voice totally changed emotionally, "Oh … the glass business," he quietly said. His voice slowed down and he couched his words. I now knew that the glass business was an emotional tug for him and I needed to find out why.

If I had just read the earnings report, I would not have heard the CEO's tone of voice change. This turned out to be the key to this project. Lesson learned: **Listen** to earnings calls!

I decided to call the analyst who'd asked this question in hopes of learning why the CEO stayed in glass. The analyst told me the CEO's father had acquired the glass business, so he was holding onto it for emotional reasons. I would never have assumed that was the reason. Another lesson learned for me. Don't assume decisions are made rationally. Sometimes, they aren't.

Now, I had to tell my client. My client knew the competitor's CEO personally and played golf with him. Yet he did not know that he was holding onto the glass business for emotional reasons. I concluded that only an event outside the CEO's control would drive him out of glass, and I hoped it wouldn't be an accident at the glass plant. I recommended that he closely monitor his competitor's activity for such an event.

A couple of years passed by without any change until a group of influential stockholders presented the company with a lawsuit to sell off the losing glass business since it was dragging down the company's earnings. The stockholders won the lawsuit and

Don't assume decisions are made rationally. Sometimes they're not.

the company divested its glass business. And my client was ready to capture this company's glass business.

Stress and Anxiety

In a similar vein your words or actions may have unintended or unhelpful effects. How do you correct this right on the spot or can you?

Maybe he's unexpectedly stressed during your conversation. When I notice this, I often remark, "It looks like you're very busy," versus saying that you look stressed. Depending on his response,

I might ask if he'd like to reschedule our call. Sometimes he perks up and we continue. Other times he'll tell me about his circumstances, and then we'll talk or we'll reschedule. The other person is always grateful that I am willing to listen to his circumstance.

Case Study: Stress

I interviewed two gentlemen from a leading university who used my client's services. My client was looking for their opinions about the company's product line; how well the products worked for them; where the gaps were; what services the institution would use in the future; and where they saw the industry going.

One of the men started to criticize the very senior person who had hired me. He couldn't say anything nice about the company and was rude about it. Each time he finished talking he quickly hit mute and his eyes were glaring. The other gentleman had more constructive thoughts initially, but as his colleague was so abrasive and critical, he became quieter and his eyes almost glazed over. The conversation did not end on a happy note.

I had just finished my writeup from this conversation when I got sidetracked by my husband to go for a cross-country ski before dark. When I got back to my work after dinner, there was an email from this rude complainer. He apologized for his behavior and told me what he had shared was not how he felt. He had just received a bad work performance review from his boss and his reporting people didn't have good things to say about him either. He shared what he really thought about my client's company, which was constructive and helpful, and offered to have another conversation. I was grateful that I had not sent the original writeup to my client.

Distractions

Perhaps the other person is distracted during your conversation since he's multitasking or there is background noise that makes it hard to hear each other. I resent it when people multitask during our conversation. Unfortunately, it's increasingly common. I will stop talking when I see multitasking in play. Usually, the multi-tasker takes the hint and stops.

When there is too much noise, I'll ask to reschedule the call unless it's just for a short duration. Once I was unwittingly the guilty party. I had given a webinar from my car at Denver's City Park as we had lost our Internet connection about an hour before the webinar was scheduled. We were in the Q&A portion right at the end. It had gone without a snag, and I was breathing a sigh of relief. Suddenly, the city's nearby tornado siren went off and it was deafening. I could not escape it! That was the end of the Q&A since the siren went on for a full minute. At least it was at the very end. I redeemed myself somewhat by answering the remaining questions in a blog.

Make sure you have enough sleep to be alert.

Forgetting

What if you forget or lack some crucial information that would lend credibility to your conversation?

This has happened to me more than once when I was tired. Those were hard lessons learned. Make sure you have enough sleep to be alert. This can also happen when you're feeling anxious or stressed out. I suffered from that more in my earlier days. Now I work on being grounded through breathing exercises or meditation, so I usually don't feel too stressed out to engage in a conversation. I also use some of the tools described in Chapter 8, *Pre-Execution: Get Grounded.* But I still forget when I'm tired.

> **Being observant and spontaneous are two essential skills of a good conversationalist.**

Awkwardness

What if you respond awkwardly in the moment or break from your planned conversation? This happens most often when I have misjudged the person's preferred communication style. I can usually recover when I notice how he's reacting. Being observant and spontaneous are two essential skills of a good conversationalist. I've often learned some valuable information when I have diverted from my planned conversation. Don't worry. You can return to your planned conversation. You don't know what you don't know, and you need to be open to learning this.

Question or Comment

You want to keep the conversation flowing so it's good to think about having a good balance between asking him a question, commenting on what he said or sharing something with him. You might ask for clarification and understanding.

Be considerate and clear. Ask only one question at a time. If you ask two questions, she is likely to only answer one of them. You might run out of time or forget to return to the one that didn't get answered. Worse yet, she might answer the question you didn't care as much about, at length.

Note that 55% of the communication is outside the words you say. According to Albert Mehrabian, a researcher of body language, communication is 55% nonverbal, 38% vocal, and 7% words only. Whether you believe these percentages, this breakdown illustrates that reading another person during a conversation is complex. If you're not on a video call, your voice and words are all the communication you have. So, you need to be even more observant of the tone and pitch of his voice, and how it changes. You need to listen to how her breathing and speaking change.

In your intensity to observe the other person, you can often forget that she is reading you too. Remember you're communicating your body language, breathing, voice and words with the other person.

While people often repeat the other person's words, mimicking facial expressions can make the other person feel the interaction was more positive. Also, when you mimic the other person's facial or other body expressions, it can help you understand the emotions she is feeling.

your turn

What have you learned when you realized your assumptions were wrong?

How do you deal with stress, whether it's yours or the other person's?

What have some of your moments of awkwardness been during a conversation?

What have you learned from them?

Be careful to ask only one question at a time.

And remember, the other person is reading your body language and speech.

Advances are made by answering questions.
Discoveries are made by questioning answers.

—**Bernard Haisch,** American Astrophysicist

chapter seventeen

Execute: Listen to the Response

People can tell when you aren't listening
and are waiting to have your say.

Listening takes courage. Whenever you listen thoroughly to someone else's ideas, you open yourself up to the possibility that some of your assumptions or ideas are wrong. Listen actively to what's being said. Patiently let him finish expressing his thoughts. Recognition is a deep human need. When you acknowledge the other person's point of view during a conversation, it is like being a testimonial to it. By recognizing him, you create a climate for agreement and more information sharing.

Most people listen at only 25% effi-ciency. On average, we speak 125 words

It takes practice to be a good listener.

per minute and think three to four times faster. It takes discipline and practice to put your thoughts and needs aside and to focus all your attention on what the other person is saying … and might be thinking or feeling.

Good listeners use that gap to think about what's been said and weigh the speaker's comments against other knowledge. They listen for what was not said or not well articulated.

It takes practice to be a good listener—to listen generously. By being a good listener, you convey you have heard what she's said, have found it to be interesting, and would like to hear more and appreciate the sharing. Listening shows respect and caring for the other person.

People can tell when you aren't listening and are waiting to have your say. Put your talking ego on hold. Note: if you have an idea to share based on what he's saying, and struggle to remember it for when the time is right, come up with a technique or strategy that will become your memory trigger. It could be as simple as writing a key word on a sticky note pad.

Sometimes, I write down my thoughts during a conversation so I don't forget them, in case one or two of them are good ideas to bring up later in the conversation. I just don't want to interrupt the other person's flow.

I like these snippets by Malcolm Gladwell, the author of *The Tipping Point* and *Talking to Strangers*. They were taken from *The Diary of a CEO* podcast with Gladwell and Steven Bartlett that can be found on YouTube:

"You can't be a good journalist unless you have a kind of baseline respect for what others can teach you. If you're going to be a good interviewer, you must enter into every interview with the expectation that you know less … that the person you're interviewing has something to tell you … to trust that this person can ultimately teach me something that I can't learn on my own … that requires an assertion of humility."

As Gladwell says, in normal conversation we have an urge to assert ourselves and we think we have an intellectual or information advantage. Interruptions are often the other person asserting superiority about a point. You must turn that off in yourself if you want to be an effective interviewer.

Here is a list of what you can think about as you're listening to the other person. Thinking this way will help you be a better listener.

- Is it clear what he means?
- Is that answer relevant to the question?
- Is the answer complete?
- What does that tone of voice mean?
- Why is she suddenly speaking so quickly?
- Why did her expression change just now?
- Why did she just take such a deep breath?
- Why did she suddenly go quiet?
- Why is he trying to change the subject?
- Why isn't she answering my question?
- What isn't she saying?
- Is what he just said accurate?
- Should I comment now, probe or be silent?
- Does she have a different energy level that was not there before?

Lay Aside Your Preconceived Notions

Truthiness is what you want the facts to be,
as opposed to what the facts are.
—**Stephen Colbert,** American Comedian, TV Host and Author

Biased expectations are conversational blind spots. All too often you assume that others see, hear, feel and think how you think. They probably don't.

People like you to treat them the way they like to be treated, which is not necessarily the way you like to be treated. Try to put yourself in their shoes as much as you can. Your objective is to be so attuned to the other person that you feel like you're sitting with her in person instead of on a phone call or video chat. And so does she.

Researchers report that you drop out of conversations every 12-18 seconds to process what people are saying, which leads you to:

- Hear what you **expect** to hear.

- Hear what you **want** to hear.

- **Let your internal thoughts be what you are hearing** instead of what she is saying.

You are making sense of what you are **hearing based on your experience,** which may not match where the other person is going in the conversation. In the same vein, the person you are talking with also has his biases.

Biases

> We do not see things as they are,
> we see them as we are.
> —**The Talmud**

Here are two examples of my biases. I was hired to collect competitive intelligence at a trade show in the demolition industry, which was absolutely the most fun trade show I've ever worked. My client told me that the gentleman showcasing a key competitor's equipment would be tough and hard-nosed.

I was fearful and dreaded meeting him and postponed meeting him until the end of the day. I had visited three other competitors by then and had built up my nerve. I hoped that he'd be less tough at the end of the day since he would be tired. I also wanted to have him to myself, which I thought would be more likely late in the day. I was right.

For some reason, he was pleasant and nice to me. He showed me everything I needed to know and invited me to see a product demo the next day. It was held outside as this was heavy duty equipment that you could not demonstrate indoors. Seeing all this cool equipment being demon-

Biased expectations are conversational blind spots.

strated was the most fun I'd had in a long time at a trade show as I slipped into the required protective wear: a hard hat, safety glasses and an orange safety vest.

This incident was a reminder that I need to be more aware of my biases. While I appreciated being appraised about him from my client, I let fear from someone else's perspective make me anxious and drive me instead of meeting and deciding for myself.

In another instance, I was biased to think that companies never lose solely due to their price. It's always part of decision-making but not the only factor. But I was proven wrong in this Win/Loss project.

My client budgeted for 100 interviews, which I thought seemed extreme given that its product was a commodity. But they were losing market share so rapidly and were desperate to know why. After 10 interviews, pricing was clearly the reason. Their price was much higher than any of their competitors, and for a commodity where there was no justification. That was the sole reason they were losing share.

Competition consistently came in at a significantly lower price and the product was electricity. Electric power had recently been deregulated in their region, so suddenly there was a flurry of competitors. This monopoly provider had not adjusted its pricing for competition! I never dreamt this would be the reason when I took on the project.

What Else ...

Another question I like to ask in customer interviews, which also works well in research or sales calls to help counter bias is:

> *What haven't I asked you that you would like to share*
> *with me? Or that I should know?*

Or asked another way, what haven't we talked about that's important to you?

I want the other person to realize that I cannot guess or know what she wants to tell me during our conversation. In addition, this kind of question leads me to learn what I don't know since I didn't think to ask about it. Most importantly, I want to let her know I am listening and I want to hear what's on her mind.

In one Win/Loss call I asked, "What else would you like to tell me?" The IT manager told me that a key strength of the winning competitor's sales team was that they demonstrated how other customers' operations had improved by using their software. That way, he could more clearly see how the competitor's technology would work for his company. My client's company did not include this in their product demo. They just demonstrated how their software would work for the IT manager's company. What a great action item to get from a Win/Loss interview. This was inserted into the sales process as part of the product demo going forward.

your turn

Challenge: Improve Your Listening.

Here is a simple exercise to learn how you are perceived as a listener.

Answer the first few questions before you ask your colleagues for their honest, constructive answers. Be prepared to be criticized. Be curious and open to learning.

1. How good a listener do you think you are? Why?
2. What do you do well as a listener?
3. Where could you improve your listening skills?
4. What are some of the ways you let others know you're listening?

Ask some colleagues.

1. How good a listener do you think I am?
2. Why do you feel this way about my listening? Evidence?
   - Is there anything that stands out in my listening habits?
   - What do you think I do well as a listener?
   - How could I improve as a listener?
3. How do you know I'm listening to you?
   - Have you noticed when I'm not listening?
   - How did that make you feel?

You will know when you have asked enough people. You will observe some trends, and you can take action to improve your listening. Good luck!

**We have two ears and one mouth
so that we can listen twice as much as we speak.**

—**Epictetus,** Philosopher (over 2,000 years ago)

chapter eighteen

Execute: Deception, Misinformation, Omission

There is no single behavior
that is indicative of deception—not one.

Most are aware of the terms *fake news* and *fake videos*, something that became a new norm post 2020. You want to be on guard against deception during a conversation—any conversation. Deceptive people are looking for ways to manage your perception for what they are talking about … and how you respond.

Remember, you can think much faster than you speak, so people have time to think to deceive you if that is the path they take, but happily they usually do not. Most people are honest during business conversations and just tell white lies or social lies. But people do lie just often enough that you need to be aware of how people behave when trying to deceive you.

In my experience, it's often hard to say exactly what makes me feel like someone is lying to me. I just have that feeling.

Deception is a very difficult human behavior to detect. Most people, both laypersons and professionals, are not very good at detecting lies according to Joe Navarro, former FBI Agent, author of *What Every BODY Is Saying* and founder of the Body Language Institute. Most just have a 50:50 chance of accurate detection, while experts get it right about 60% of the time. Even Dr. Paul Ekman, deception detection expert, says there is no single behavior that is indicative of deception—not one.

Navarro suggests that you observe when the other person becomes uncomfortable during your conversation. People tend to be more relaxed and show comfortable nonverbals when they are telling the truth. You want to establish what that looks like as you start your conversation and put the other person at ease. That way you know what the other person looks like and sounds like when he's comfortable.

You show discomfort when you don't like what you are seeing, hearing, or talking about things that you'd rather not talk about. Physiologically your heart pace quickens, you breathe faster and you perspire more. Some people blush and others might go pale. You automatically move your body to attempt to block or distance yourself from your situation.

Deception is a very difficult human behavior to detect.

These are sudden changes, some of which I shared in Chapter 15, *Observe Verbal and Nonverbal Communication for Cues.*

Verbal and Nonverbal Signs of Discomfort

- Pupil dilation
- Loss of eye contact
- Touching the eyes or brow
- Eye blink increase

- Eyelid flutter
- Eye blocking
- Eye squinting
- Rolling eyes
- Jutting jaw
- Tucked chin
- Furrowed brow
- Speeded breathing
- Exhaling heavily, noticeably blowing out air
- Clearing throat
- Hard swallows/dry throat
- Hesitant or uninflected speech
- Lip biting, compression or pursing
- Lip licking
- Mouth quivers or squirms
- Tongue jutting
- Covering or touching the neck
- Squeezing face
- Stroke back of head with hand
- Change of posture: leaning away from you
- Twisting and intertwining hands
- Cracking knuckles
- Crossing and uncrossing legs nervously
- Body trembling

- Hands disappear or grip chair arms
- Outstretched hands raised palms up
- Half shrugs or shoulders hunched up to occupy less space
- Hand pushing hair back
- Playing with necklace, watch or other jewelry
- Pulling jacket closed or adjusting collar or tie

But these actions don't necessarily mean the person is lying. He might just be stressed, scared or nervous about something you said. She might not like you or is uncomfortable with you. Perhaps he is suffering from some event or condition that is troubling, which he can't let go of during your conversation.

But, if your conversation has been going along smoothly with relaxed nonverbal motions, and you notice such a sudden behavior change during your conversation, you will want to probe to learn what's behind it. Your objective during the conversation is to elicit the information you seek.

Navarro suggests that liars are usually troubled by three things:

> Hearing a question they don't like; processing that question and coming up with a suitable answer; and answering the question, (known as) vocalizing.

Liars seldom touch or engage with you physically. They seem to be stiffer than you'd expect. Some will lock eyes with you to convince you they're not lying. If a headshake or head movement isn't synchronous with what he is saying, but follows it, then he might be lying. Or if she is saying something in the affirmative but shaking her head no, this might indicate deception. Likewise, if he is saying no to something but shaking his head yes, you must wonder.

Experts like Navarro say that liars often don't think about the presentation of their

Their presentation lacks the commitment you observe and hear in an honest conversation.

lie, just the words, but not the body movement or word emphasis that takes place in a normal conversation. The tone or pitch of the voice might not fit the words they're saying. It might feel more like they're reciting to you rather than telling you their story with some conviction.

They might be overly dramatic in their presentation. Or they might be stiff when usually they use their hands while speaking. Perhaps they talk with their mouths covered or present a thoughtful deliberate stance as though they're thinking about what to say next, rather than emphasizing the point they're making with the proper intonation. Their presentation lacks the commitment you observe and hear in an honest conversation.

Potential Deceptive Verbal Behaviors

Below are a few behaviors to tip you off to suspect deception:

- Failure to answer or even understand a simple question.
- Overly specific answers that provide more information than you asked for but don't answer your question.
- Long-winded answers delivered when Yes or No would do.
- Avoid facts in his answer.
- An inappropriate level of politeness is injected that appears to be phony.

- When she asks a question back to your question, pushing the conversation off track.

- Inconsistent statements are interjected into the conversation.

- Doesn't answer your question or pushes it off to another person.

Joe Navarro sums it up nicely:

> It's not so much a nonverbal, but it's the people who are trying hard to convince you … or there is too much drama, when no drama is needed. Most honest people convey things once, and that's it.

How to Probe

When I suspect deception, I probe with short statements or questions.

- Tell me more ….

- What else?

- Who else?

- I don't understand.

- I'm confused.

- What makes you say that?

This speeds up the conversation and makes it harder for him to keep lying. It takes her away from prepared comments if that's how she operates. I also might find out she isn't lying, but she just doesn't know the answer to what I am looking for. I need to find another source.

Phrases That Raise Suspicion

Some phrases tip me off if they are said in a more manipulative way or defensively.

- I would never do a thing like that. (Worse yet if they're nodding their head in the affirmative)

- I would never say something like that.

- I'm not sure I'm the right person for you to speak with.

- Gee, I'm not sure if I can answer that.

- To be perfectly honest ….

For the first two phrases, the person is not answering your question, which is usually a Yes or No question. You must wonder why not.

The next two statements can be sincere if they are said at the start of your conversation, since maybe she is not the right person since she lacks knowledge about the topic and doesn't want to waste your time. If your conversation has been moving at a certain pace and she decides to avoid the question, there is a reason. It could be deception, omission or simply discomfort as to where the conversation is going. As a conversationalist, you need to put on your intuitive radar and figure this out!

One phrase I despise is, "To be perfectly honest …" If you are being honest with me there is no need to say this. I do have one friend who says this in everyday conversation and she is being honest with me. This is another reminder that you need to understand people's speech habits.

Does Someone's Sharing Disposition Change?

When I suspect deception or purposeful omission, I look to see if his sharing disposition changes. This can be another red flag. Or it might be an opportunity to change my tact and take the conversation in a new direction.

Sharing Disposition

Egocentric	Deeply Intelligent	Nerd	Helper
Motor Mouth	Intellectual	Clam	Evasive Deceptive

(More detail in Chapter 11, *Pre-Execution: Communication Style.*)

Or does his sharing slow or almost stop when it had been flowing so naturally? You must wonder what's up. Maybe he realizes he has shared too much. Or he might simply be pausing to think.

As Navarro and other experts tell us, detecting deception is so difficult, even for trained experts. I prefer the approach of asking more questions and probing, especially when I notice the other person's discomfort. I'm looking for information first and foremost versus spending too much energy trying to discern if he is telling me the truth. Yet, I don't ignore it if I suspect it.

your turn

Have you felt you were deceived during a conversation?

What made you feel you had been deceived?

How did you react?

Would you react differently next time?

**He who permits himself to tell a lie once,
finds it much easier to do it a second and third time,
till at length it becomes habitual.**

—Thomas Jefferson

chapter nineteen

Execute:
Be Visually Friendly

Mirror the body language of the person
you're talking with to make him feel comfortable.

With the increasing use of video calls, you can read more of the
body, at least the head, neck and shoulders and hands if she uses
them. Avoid distractions so you're focused on the other person's
signals. It is extremely important that any signal you send appears
natural and not overdone.

Be attractive, appropriate for the conversation you're having.
Don't be unkempt during video conferences. Period. It makes a
bad impression. Always.

Barriers to a connection may include some body motions:

- Leaning away from the other person

- Using objects as obstacles

- Any attempt to block your body or chest

- Crossing arms (although not always)

Visually there are some red flag behaviors to avoid:

- Invasion of private space

- Staring

- Eye rolling

- Touching aside from a handshake or customary greeting stance

- Wrinkling of eyebrows

- Exaggerated raising or lowering of eyebrows

Ideally, you want to mirror the body language of the person you're talking with to make him feel comfortable. While meeting in-person if you make yourself appear smaller and the other person notices, he will feel like he has the upper hand in the conversation.

A real smile improves your humor and attitude since it releases endorphins.

Positive Visual Behaviors

Following are visual behaviors that usually make the other person feel more comfortable during your conversation. Be authentic: if you're a fake, the other person usually can see right through you.

Smile: Stress Reduction
A true smile reveals the corners of the mouth and the wrinkles around the eyes, like in laughter. A true smile lets the other person see and feel that you're happy, enthusiastic and open. A smile from you is even felt when it's unseen in an audio call. A real smile improves your humor and attitude since it releases endorphins. Smile even if you're faking it, to reduce your stress and the other person's too.

On the other hand, be aware that when a person sees a forced smile, she can tell it's not genuine. It may have the opposite effect of a true smile since she may feel like you're manipulating the conversation. When you frown, grimace or have negative expressions, your body releases cortisol, which raises stress levels. You don't want this since your stress often gets transmitted to the other person.

Mimic

One reason I like to mimic the other person's nonverbal expression is to understand the emotions he might be experiencing. Mimicking facial expressions makes the other person feel the interaction was more positive. We often mirror the other person's words, but this is even more powerful assuming your conversation is video or in-person. Mimic his breathing. You can observe it by looking at how his shoulders rise and fall. If she has long hair you can notice how her hair moves.

While you can't mimic the other person's nonverbal expression on an audio call, you can mimic their breathing if you listen closely. You can also mirror or paraphrase the other person's words.

Use Hands

Using your hands helps people understand your message. Italians almost execute another dialog with their hands. I notice that using my hands helps me feel

more confident and authentic since this is part of who I am. You can use your hands to punctuate certain words and phrases for effect and fall into a better rhythm. Loosen up and don't think about your hands. Hands help you express yourself better and to stay focused if that is naturally how you express yourself.

Bow Slightly

When you incline your head forward slightly as you greet someone, it shows deference and humility and helps remove any perceived status differences. Tilt your head forward slightly, smile and make eye contact to show you're honored and happy to meet him. He is likely to be happy to meet you. When a person leans forward during a conversation it usually means he is engaged.

Take an Angle

When what you have to say will make the other person feel challenged, shift your feet to stand or sit at an angle. That makes this type of conversation less adversarial.

Leaning your head slightly to the left or right is perceived by others as a friendly gesture. The carotid arteries that carry oxygenated blood to the brain are exposed when you tilt your head, signaling that you do not feel the need to protect yourself. A person who leans his head is perceived as trustworthy and friendly. It shows the other person that you're relaxed about this conversation, which he often mimics.

Problem Solver

You need to know people's habits with crossed arms. Crossing arms helps you stick with a difficult problem longer and helps perform better on solvable problems. But be aware that some people sit this way when they're not open to your message. You may feel like they are ignoring you. But sometimes they cross their arms when they're cold.

Encourage

A simple head nod can be quite encouraging at the right time in a conversation to show that you agree or understand a certain point. It also shows you're listening. Some people continually nod their heads when they agree with what you're saying. I often wonder if they're really listening when they continually nod, so be aware of that too.

Raising your eyebrows slightly up and down a fraction of a second is seen as friendly and encouraging.

your turn

Be aware of how your body motions can encourage sharing.

Practice the friendly poses discussed here and use them during your conversations.

Do you notice that these body positions encourage sharing?

Be aware of those body positions or motions that are barriers to connecting.

Sometimes you can get in those less friendly positions unintentionally. Be aware of this.

**Your body language shapes
who you are.**

—**Amy Cuddy**

chapter twenty

Execute:
Probe the Response

Knowing when and how to probe
or NOT to probe is an art that loosens lips.

Knowing when to probe is an important skill. After all, you have limited time for your conversation. You want to hone in on the areas that are most important to probe. For example, I was conducting a customer retention conversation. Clearly the main issue was poor customer service. During one conversation, I collected four different examples of poor customer service by probing.

Match their pace of speech and expression.

To carry this a step further, poor customer service was a key issue in all my retention and churn calls for this company. As a result of these findings, this company integrated its customer service and customer success operations to improve internal communication and communication with their customers.

Below are some ideas to help you probe efficiently and effectively.

Passive Probes: Hmm … I see … OK … uh huh …. (deadpan facial expression)

Responsive: Really …. How Interesting! (animated facial expression)

Responsive: Acknowledge the other person's point. Repeat it to encourage more ….

Mirroring: Repeating or paraphrasing what was said.

Developing: Tell me more about …. Help me understand. What do you mean by that?

Developing: Can we go back and talk about …? What is your experience doing …?

Developing: Fill in the blank inquiries or statements. Statement … uh …

I know you said that the new product was in development at the lab in uh … ___ .

Clarifying: So, you mean ….Yes? What do you think about this?

Confronting: I'm totally confused. How could this be true?

Changing: Moving right along …. I don't mean to change the subject, but …

Diverging: You said what? Really … did you mean it?

Mirroring: Repeating/Paraphrasing – Repeat core words or concepts to encourage a person to expand on what he said. Also, to make sure that you understood what he meant. Oftentimes, when people hear me repeat their words, they'll change things around a bit. I don't usually use their exact words, but something similar. I don't want to be a guilty parrot, which some people see right through and can feel manipulated.

For example, price often comes up in my Win/Loss interviews as one of several important factors in a company's decision-making process. Later in the conversation, I'll remind them of what they mentioned about price earlier to see if they'll provide more detail about pricing. Typically, they provide more detail than they did previously. Such as, "Actually it was less important than having the right product features." Or "We were willing to pay more since the company provides great customer service." Then you can probe for more details about customer service and how it merits a higher price.

Match their pace of speech and expression. Usually, they won't even notice this, but it often makes people feel comfortable. Other ways to mirror: voice tone, cadence, inflection, volume, word choice.

Developing - Completion inquiries or fill-in-the-blank inquiries (FITB). Unresolved questions or statements designed to get the other person to provide the answer. I remember my father's use of Whatchamacallit.

So far, I hear the top candidate they'll hire as CEO is someone like John Nichols.

Or what was his name?

Or more like ….

Or probably more like … uh ….

They might answer, "More like Ted Frazer, but we're also considering Alice Gunderson."

Clarifying – I use this when a person is describing something technical that I'm not following, or if I couldn't hear him or her. This can also be due to a poor connection or a thick accent!

Confronting – Another word that works well with a challenging tone of voice is "Really?"

Changing – In Win/Loss, retention or churn calls, this is especially useful when he complains about customer service or vents. You acknowledge this, ask how to make it better, make a note of it and move on.

Diverging – You said their presales team wasn't so good, but yet they won the business. Did you mean that?

Sometimes when you probe you learn things you weren't looking for. You might learn that the person is coming from a very different place than you thought. You need to be open to this. For example, I had scheduled a Loss call with a customer located in France. The Account Executive (AE) told me that his company was a finalist for the business and that a key competitor had won the business. Sadly, he also told me that the potential customer had stopped communicating with him, so I was skeptical that she would take my call. She almost immediately agreed to the call.

Remember, every person you talk to can potentially provide you with the information you seek.

I learned that my client was not a finalist for the business, and another service provider won the deal that the AE hadn't even mentioned as a contender. As a result, I had some different questions that were not part of the Win/Loss script, although I hadn't expected this turn of events.

We learned some things about the winner that we didn't know, most particularly that they had implemented inventory management software for this customer, and it integrated well with the software solution that the competitor had pitched. My client didn't even know that this competitor offered an inventory management software solution.

Note: Many of these probing skills are also elicitation techniques—the focus of Part Two of *Loosen Their Lips*.

Conclude on a Positive Note

You want to have a goal for how the conversation will end, that is meeting your specific goals for this business conversation. Connected to that, decide how you'd like to leave the other person feeling at the end of your conversation. As mentioned earlier, I have an intention of kindness. I want to leave the person feeling better at the end of our conversation than when we said "Hello."

As I conclude my calls, I often share a summary of what she shared that was most helpful, especially those points I'd love to have her expound on. Many is the conversation I've ended this way, and she has this need to either emphasize the same points, provide more detail on some issues or give me some new information.

I answer people's questions about who I am and why I'm calling at the start of a conversation. However, depending on how the call went and what type of call it is, I'll also conclude with, "Are there any questions you have for me?" just before I end the conversation. I want them to feel that I'm being transparent.

Remember, every person you talk to can potentially provide you with the information you seek or at least some of it. And that person can also lead you to other resources.

- Thank you so much and ….
- Do you know someone else who knows about this who might be willing to talk with me? (Extra credit if they offer to introduce me to him.)

- Perhaps there is an association you might refer me to.

- Do you recommend any magazines, news resources, media influencers or blogs on this subject?

A "Thank You" goes a long way. "This was so helpful. Is it OK if I get back in touch with you in case I need to get clarification once I've reviewed my notes from our conversation?" I've never had anyone refuse me. Most people generously offer that I am welcome to reach back to them any time without my asking them.

If you compensate him financially for his time, let him know how that will happen. Or perhaps you're donating to a charity on her behalf. Remind her of this arrangement. This makes a good impression when you remember the financial angle as promised. She appreciates that you valued her time and feedback.

your turn

Practice probing. What is your tendency with probing? Sometimes, I probe too much. Other times I make assumptions and probe less. When I listen to the recording of conversations where I've probed less, I often realize that I missed an opportunity to ask a few more questions.

Make sure to conclude on a positive note and express gratefulness for the other person's time and sharing. You will stand out these days if you're polite. It's sad but true.

**Probing the other person's response
encourages elaboration
and keeps the conversation flowing.**
—Ellen Naylor

chapter twenty-one

Analyze:
Analyze the Call

If you don't evaluate your call or customer visit,
you're missing the opportunity to plan for the next one!

Evaluate the Response

Evaluate the reliability of the person as a source as well as the data he has provided. This is a good time to review "Assessing the reliability and validity of your Friendlies," even though not all the people you interview are what Professor Jonathan Calof refers to as Friendlies. For more details, see Chapter 6, *Plan: Research: The Collection Continuum: Human Sources.*

What is relevant from this conversation towards meeting your data collection goals?

- Was your planning adequate?

- Did you do the right research?

- Did you learn anything? If so, what?

- Did it fill in some gaps of knowledge? What else do you still need to learn?

- Do you need to rephrase, eliminate or add some questions based on what you learned?

How did the person's bias affect what he told you? Is his bias so strong that it discredits what you learned? Can you factor out the biases?

Then, ask yourself:

- Did you get enough information to complete your project from this conversation?

- Can you factor in what you learned from this conversation with other resources to complete your project?

- As a result of the conversation, do you need to talk to another person(s)? If so, identify the person(s) or research to find other sources to speak with.

- Did you receive accurate information?

- Why do you feel you did or didn't get accurate information?

- Were there inconsistencies in this person's responses?

Some people intentionally deceive. Others are distorted by strong prejudices, are misinformed, or have a bad memory.

Sometimes the person you are communicating with is cooperative to a fault, such that you feel it's too good to be true. If you're feeling that way, you're probably right.

Analyze Your Behavior

Now that you've concluded your conversation, how effective were you? Did you behave ethically? How do you think you left the person feeling at the end of your conversation?

I recall an unpleasant experience I had at the conclusion of a conversation. This was with a potential business partner. I had driven one hour to a coffee shop for this meeting to discuss how we wanted to proceed. He greeted me warmly and we talked over coffee for about 30 minutes. I excused myself to visit the restroom. When I returned, he was on his mobile phone ... except that he wasn't. He was faking it. I took the hint and simply waved good-bye and left. I felt used. I never heard from him again. I wondered how I hadn't seen this coming. I had misjudged the potential relationship terribly.

Sometimes you dominate the call too much or are guilty of sucking infor-mation out of the person you are speaking

Many people don't analyze how the call went. Big mistake.

with in such a way that she feels used like I did. I was attempting to develop a business relationship and realized that the feeling was not mutual, not even close.

I listen to some recordings of my conversations to identify where or how I could have learned more. This helps me locate what I forgot to ask. Those I speak with are OK with me getting back in touch. The downside is this takes precious time that I might not have. I know I can use software or AI to record and analyze calls. But I like to listen to some calls and use my brain to learn how I can improve!

If you were with a coworker during the conversation, ask him for feedback about how well you did, and what you could have done differently. What went well? Did you hog the conversation either at the expense of your coworker or the person or people at your meeting? Provide your coworker with feedback from your perspective. Make this a learning experience. Consider how you might change things for the next time.

We all notice different things. I recall in my sales days that my tech person and I tended to observe similar things at customers' sites. This helped us be sensitive to their culture as we inched toward closing sales. In the meantime, our admin noticed all the details of what the customers said they needed, details that my tech and I often missed. As a result, we were an effective team since we noticed different things and discussed our findings to decide on the next steps together.

Next Steps and Sharing

What are the next steps, if there are next steps, to get the data you seek? Consider the Collection Continuum. Do you need to go back to the Internet or social media to get more clarification, find ideas, or find others to talk to?

> **It's important to establish lasting relationships and not always expect interactions to yield immediate results.**

Share your responses with those who need to know. Include your confidence level and the date if your software doesn't automatically date stamp. Or share an analysis of what you've discovered, what's important and why. Make recommendations for future steps and action if appropriate.

Patience is a virtue. It's important to establish lasting relationships and not always expect interactions to yield immediate results. I like the words of wisdom from Seena Sharp, author of *Competitive Intelligence Advantage.* "Occasionally, you'll get what you need quickly. More often, it requires far more effort and time than anyone acknowledges, especially in today's immediate results world."

your turn

Many people don't analyze how the call or customer visit went. Big mistake. Do it! Especially if you record calls or if a colleague accompanied you on the call or customer visit.

Have you learned what you hoped for during the call?

Do you feel the information you collected is accurate?

What are the gaps that remain, if any?

How did you come across?

Were you adequately grounded?

Did you adapt yourself to how they like to communicate?

Once you analyze what you learned from the other person and about yourself, it's time to move forward.

How will you execute the next call?

Do you need to do some more research?

How would you rate the person you spoke with as a future source? Make a note of it and move on.

**Evaluate the response by its relevance,
completeness and validity.**

—Ellen Naylor

PART TWO

Elicitation

Using elicitation techniques effectively
are a conversationalist's superpower!

—Ellen Naylor

chapter twenty-two

Elicitation Introduction

Elicitation is a conversation that induces
people to tell you things without you asking.

Why do I have a separate section on elicitation techniques?
They fit right into the business conversation preparation, pre-execution, execution and analysis process shared thus far. In the first part of *Loosen Their Lips*, I focused on developing and asking the right questions, and listening closely to answers. Elicitation techniques build from what you are already doing, if you're following the steps to conduct an effective conversation as outlined in this book.

What's unique about elicitation is that you're not asking questions to get the information you seek. You're uncovering the information you are looking for through conversation, not questions. Yet, you are getting answers to the questions that you or your client have.

I like to use elicitation techniques as they flow nicely in a business conversation. I find they come naturally since they are based on human nature. When I first learned about them, I was surprised that they were used to manipulate conversation. Then I discovered that they were developed by the intelligence community for the kind of conversations that are more challenging and have dire consequences if things go badly. I haven't been part of the intelligence community, but business conversations are far less risky than the conversations and interrogations that the intelligence community engages in.

Definition and Practice

Elicitation is a conversation that induces people to tell you things without you asking. It is a structured method of communication used to get predetermined information from people without necessarily making them aware that you are collecting it. The goal is to collect information that is not readily available and to do so without raising suspicion that specific facts are being sought.

Elicitation involves planned, conversational interaction to gather the data you seek.

We're often looking for information that's not readily available in competitive intelligence, and this is another tool you can use to be a more effective conversationalist. Some of my most appreciative students of elicitation techniques are in sales. They use these techniques as they work their way through the sales funnel.

For example, they want to uncover their potential customer's business problems so they can offer an effective solution to address them. They want to learn how to overcome all the objections the customer might have to NOT buy their solution, so they can overcome them. They want to learn the customer's decision-making process and who will be part of it. They need to learn the customer's decision-making criteria. Sales wants to learn about the competition and how they are perceived in comparison. Simply asking customers these types of questions often doesn't work.

Elicitation involves planned, conversational interaction to gather the data you seek. Conversation flows without raising the other person's concern about what he told you.

When conducted by a skilled collector, elicitation appears to be a normal social or professional conversation. The other person may not realize that he was targeted or that he provided meaningful information. I notice this happens often enough in interviewing even when not using elicitation techniques. People who just want to be helpful (Helper Sharing Disposition) as well as those who don't recognize the value of what they know (Deeply Intellectual Sharing Disposition), share readily.

Elicitation techniques work.

Elicitation avoids direct questions and encourages openness. It's conversational so it reduces concern or suspicion. It encourages the other person to speak with comfort.

Elicitation can take more time than standard interviewing— longer than just asking questions—unless you're good at elicitation, which comes with practice.

Elicitation is a powerful conversational enabler. It builds on the common sense of conducting an interview that is covered in Part One. You plan for any type of conversation whether using elicitation techniques or not. You have objectives for your conversation, steps to get there, and how you'd like the conversation to end.

Since elicitation techniques are based on human nature, I bet you're using them right now without realizing it. That's what I noticed when I was introduced to elicitation techniques by Elicitation Guru John Nolan back in the day! I included more detail about human nature in Chapter 10, *Pre-Execution: Motivation*.

Elicitation techniques can be used on the phone, email, text, in-person, or video chatting with anyone in business: customers, competitors, industry experts and fellow employees. You can use them with your kids, although I don't recommend you use them with your spouse! Elicitation techniques are a category of research tasks that use visual, verbal, or written stimuli to encourage participants to talk about their ideas or to share them digitally.

Elicitation techniques work. For business you need to consider the win/win of this process so as not to exploit your customers or other human sources of information. Remember: Intention matters. You need to be sincere and honest, not deceptive or manipulative! Your mind and heart pick up on deception and manipulation before anything else since you are programmed to protect yourself.

Questions Can Be Revealing

The reason why elicitation is conversational rather than asking questions is that people remember questions more than conversation. Questions can unintentionally reveal information about your company before you had intended, such as your company's plans, intentions and interests.

> I use elicitation techniques most often when talking to personnel at trade show booths.

Remember how much more quickly we think than we speak. When you're asking questions, the other person may be wondering …

- Who is she?

- Why is he asking?

- What's in it for me to share x, y or z?

- How shall I respond?

- How will she use what I say?

- How much should I share?

- Should I share at all?

- Is this conversation confidential?

- Will it remain confidential?

I use elicitation techniques most often when talking to personnel at trade show booths. They talk to many people and tend to remember fewer details unless your conversation was so different from anyone else's. I had that experience just once. One furniture manufacturer at the Neocon Furniture Expo remembered me from the year before since our conversation was very different from those he'd had with other attendees. We spoke about how well their furniture worked with telecom since they needed to work together. For example, how would a company's telecom connections be affected if the company moved their furniture to another floor, another building, etc. Most other attendees focused strictly on the features, look and versatility of their furniture without regard for telecom issues.

Your Relationship with the Other Person
Just as in a "normal" conversation not using elicitation techniques, you need to assess your relationship with the other person before the call. The list that follows assumes you have previously spoken with the other person. Issues around warming up the call are covered in Chapter 4, *Plan: Research: Warm Up the Interview – The Collection Continuum.*

Sharing: Yours and Theirs

- What is his attitude about sharing information?

- Likewise, motivation?

- What has he shared before?

- What was he comfortable sharing?

- What, if anything, made him clam up or look uncomfortable?

- Why would he want to share more?

- What were his questions about you or your business?

- What will you share?

Remember that while you are learning as you interview another person, the other person is sizing you up too! Elicitation often causes the other person to ask you questions since it's conversational. Asking questions makes the other person feel more powerful. So be very certain about what you are willing to share and what you don't want to share.

You don't want to give away proprietary information about your company!

Hopefully, your company has a policy about what you can share and what you can't. You don't want to give away proprietary information about your company!

If you don't have guidelines for information sharing, always share public information. If you're well informed, the other person will be learning from that. Sometimes I share information I've recently learned about a mutual competitor that's not necessarily public information and might just be a rumor. It's a great attention getter, and in my experience the other person can't help but comment.

Elicitation: A Planned Conversation

Here is what to keep in mind when planning a conversation using elicitation techniques, which is similar to planning for any conversation.

- What is your desired outcome?
- What steps will you take to get to your desired outcomes?
- How will this build on what you already know?
- What are the right conversational points you want to make, in what order?
- How will you make the conversation interesting to the other person?
- What human tendencies will you use to build your conversation thread?

This would be a good time to review Chapters 10-13: *Motivation, Communication Style, Unique: Who Is She or He? Execute the Call.*

- What is the other person's personality (5Ps)?
- What is the other person's preferred communication style?
- What is the other person's sharing disposition?
- Given all this, how do you want to come across?

When using elicitation techniques, you're adding the following to the standard conversation process:

- Macro questions/small talk questions
- Specific elicitation techniques
- More detailed planning for conversational points using elicitation techniques

**Elicitation is the bread and butter
of human intelligence —
it's the act of obtaining information.**

—**J. C. Carleson,** Former Undercover CIA Officer
and author of *Work Like a Spy*

chapter twenty-three

Elicitation:
The Process

Be silent with an extrovert who can't resist
filling in the silent gap with conversation.

Interview-Conversation-Elicitation

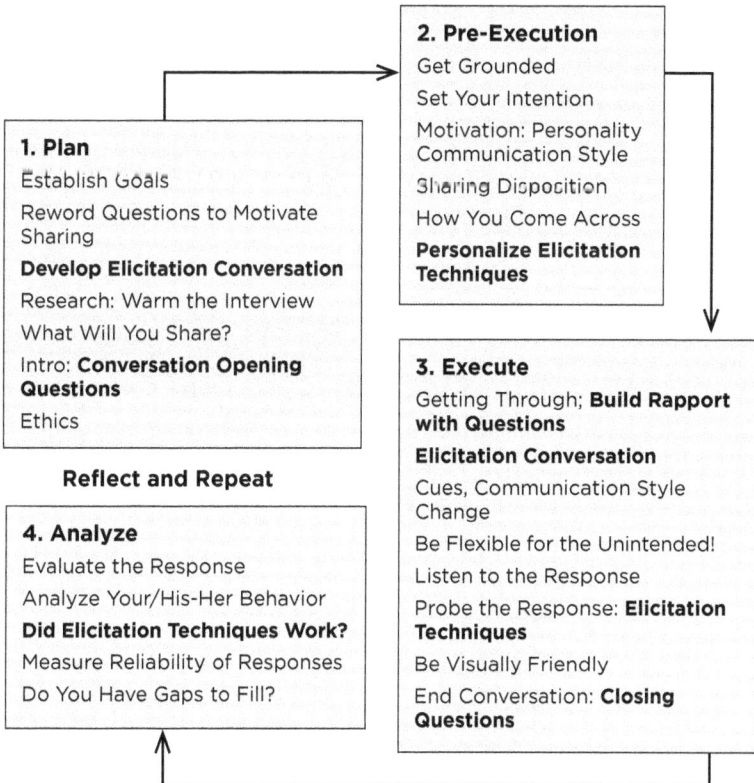

1. Plan

Establish Goals

Reword Questions to Motivate
Sharing

Develop Elicitation Conversation

Research: Warm the Interview

What Will You Share?

Intro: **Conversation Opening
Questions**

Ethics

2. Pre-Execution

Get Grounded

Set Your Intention

Motivation: Personality
Communication Style

Sharing Disposition

How You Come Across

**Personalize Elicitation
Techniques**

3. Execute

Getting Through; **Build Rapport
with Questions**

Elicitation Conversation

Cues, Communication Style
Change

Be Flexible for the Unintended!

Listen to the Response

Probe the Response: **Elicitation
Techniques**

Be Visually Friendly

End Conversation: **Closing
Questions**

Reflect and Repeat

4. Analyze

Evaluate the Response

Analyze Your/His-Her Behavior

Did Elicitation Techniques Work?

Measure Reliability of Responses

Do You Have Gaps to Fill?

1. Plan

Develop Elicitation Conversation

After you've reworded the questions to motivate sharing, you take an extra step. You need to think how to get the information during a conversation without asking questions. For example, instead of asking, "How did pricing affect your decision-making?" you might say, "These days it seems everyone is so driven by price. I just don't get it." Or, you might say, "You haven't mentioned price, so maybe it wasn't important to you." Or, "I hear that everyone's price is so close to each other's in this cutthroat business."

Conversation Opening Questions

You will develop some broad questions or small talk, which have nothing to do with the business you are asking about to build rapport. You will use them to open your conversation. You don't want to develop these on the fly. The rationale around this is that people remember questions but often forget the conversation that follows.

You want her to remember the broad questions/small talk questions, which might be more social. For example, let's say I am at a trade show approaching an exhibitor. I'll often ask how the show is going. Or ask about the weather. Other opening questions are about food, or even who they're rooting for on a major sports event that is in the news—you get the drift.

2. Pre-Execution

Personalize Collection Techniques

You'll have gone through the motivation phase of assessing his personality, communication style and sharing disposition. Think about which elicitation techniques might fit best given his personality and how you come across. Think how he might like to be treated, which might not be the same way you do. For example, don't be silent for long with an introvert other than letting him think a bit. And be silent with an extrovert who can't resist filling in the silent gap with conversation.

Most people aren't comfortable using every elicitation technique, so figure out the ones you like. One elicitation technique many people don't like is the Purposefully Erroneous Statement. I will show you how I use it, and you might decide to use it similarly. Learn which elicitation techniques seem to work with various personalities and sharing dispositions. Some of them work with all types, such as Flattery, as long as it's sincere.

As with any conversation, be adaptable when using elicitation techniques.

As with any conversation, be adaptable when using elicitation techniques. Often enough the conversation goes differently than you thought it would. Perhaps the elicitation technique you used was ineffective or worse yet made her clam up. You need to adapt quickly. I will give you an example of this from case studies as we go through the elicitation techniques in more detail in Chapters 25-29.

3. Execute

Build Rapport with Questions

Start the conversation by introducing yourself, especially if you're meeting for the first time. Then ask a general question or two that isn't related to what you want to learn. You'll have thought about a few of these questions in the Plan phase. Sometimes a news event that's just happened works well. If he hasn't read about it, most of the time he will want to know about it and will ask you for more details.

Elicitation Techniques
Then get into your conversation using the elicitation techniques that you prepared during the Plan phase. Probe her responses using elicitation techniques rather than asking more questions.

End the Conversation
Once you have completed your conversation using elicitation techniques, close with some small talk, broad questions—not unlike those you opened with. Weather is always safe, along with sports, holidays and food.

4. Analyze

Did the Elicitation Techniques Work?
Were the elicitation techniques you used effective to get the information you were looking for?

Did some of them work better than others? Are any of them to be avoided if you have a future conversation with this person?

Write the answers to the questions above in your contact database. That way you have a record of which elicitation techniques worked as they're likely to work the next time. Hopefully, you learn which one(s) didn't work so you don't make the same mistake in a future conversation.

When I have recorded these conversations, it's easy to hear what worked and what didn't. If another person listened in or was part of the meeting, we can review which elicitation techniques worked and which didn't. That's why I always include an Observer in my classes when we do elicitation role plays.

You can also use technology to transcribe your conversations, analyze how they went and how much you spoke versus the other person, for example. There is so much technology to help with transcription and analysis! Technology is a time-saver to capture trends from numerous conversations. But I still like to be low tech and listen to some of my conversations so I can pick up on verbal innuendos that I might have missed, such as changes in tone or sharing disposition at certain times during our conversation. Listening to recordings enables me to learn how I can improve my conversational skill!

chapter twenty-four

John Nolan's Elicitation Conversational Hourglass

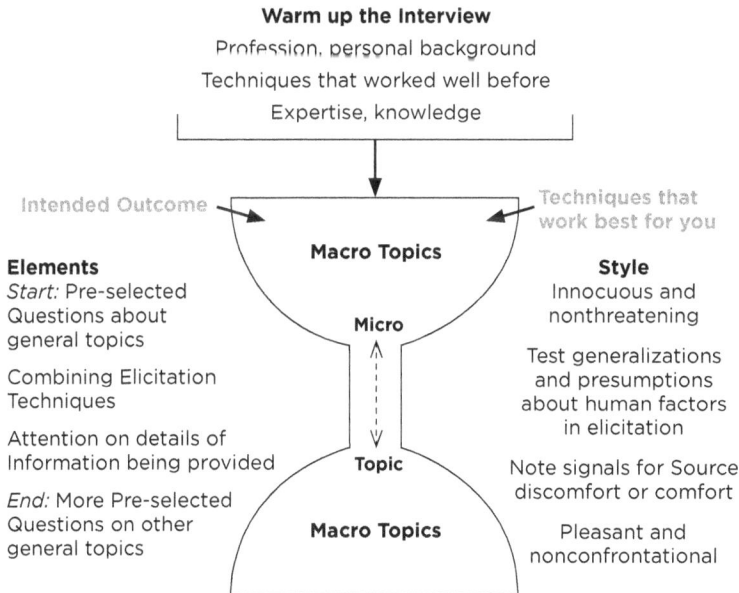

You want to concentrate on the muddle in the middle with the micro topics.

Conversational Hourglass

Warm up the Interview

Profession, personal background

Techniques that worked well before

Expertise, knowledge

Intended Outcome → | ← Techniques that work best for you

Macro Topics

Elements

Start: Pre-selected Questions about general topics

Combining Elicitation Techniques

Attention on details of Information being provided

End: More Pre-selected Questions on other general topics

Micro

∧
︙
∨

Topic

Macro Topics

Style

Innocuous and nonthreatening

Test generalizations and presumptions about human factors in elicitation

Note signals for Source discomfort or comfort

Pleasant and nonconfrontational

Paraphrased from *Confidential* ©John Nolan, p. 28

Conversational Hourglass

I showed you how elicitation techniques fit into the standard Interview—Conversation process. Now I'll describe John Nolan's Conversational Hourglass that focuses solely on elicitation. This is a great visual to plan a conversation using elicitation techniques, and how to be while conversing. It concisely shows what's included to warm up the interview and recall elicitation techniques that worked with this person previously.

If this is your first conversation with this person, you're going to be making an educated guess as to which elicitation techniques will work since you will have researched his personal background and profession prior to your conversation.

The premise behind the Conversational Hourglass is that people remember the questions at the beginning and the end of a conversation.

If you are talking with strangers at an exhibit booth, you will be approaching them with no prior research as to their personality or motivation. But you can get some ideas by watching their body motions at the exhibit booth before approaching them. If you're lucky you can eavesdrop as the booth personnel talk to another prospect. You must be extra observant and quick to pick up on a person's motivation and sharing disposition as you converse.

The premise behind the Conversational Hourglass is that people remember the beginning and the end of a conversation. They also remember questions (macro topics/small talk) more clearly and for a longer time than they do the casual elements (micro topics/what you're looking for) brought up during a conversation.

You want to prepare two sets of small talk questions (macro topics) to be used at the beginning and the end of your conversation. The other person is likely to remember these questions as they are general topics of interest that most people resonate with.

People tend to forget the "muddle in the middle," as John Nolan refers to it. You want to concentrate on the muddle in the middle with the micro topics. Intelligence from the micro topics conversation is what you're looking for. When you use elicitation techniques during this part of the conversation, the other person is apt to forget about this part of your conversation.

If the call is recorded, all bets are off if the person reviews it and/or uses AI to analyze it.

Plan and write out what steps you need to take to get the information you're looking for, including which elicitation technique you'll use for each step. This is the fun part of planning a conversation. With any conversation not using elicitation techniques, I like to draw a decision tree for how the conversation might go every step of the way so I can be flexible and spontaneous. Lastly, you want to plan how you'll conclude the micro topics part of the conversation.

Most importantly during your conversation, you will observe signals of comfort or discomfort from the other person and adjust your approach accordingly.

"The more comfortable you make someone feel, the better interview you're ultimately going to get," says interview veteran Katie Couric. And how do you make someone feel more comfortable? "Great interviewers do it by meeting subjects on their level. That means matching their mood, energy level, language style—even body language."

You will be pleasant and nonconfrontational throughout the conversation, even if you or the other person brings up some provocative topic or complains about something. You want to show empathy and compassion, which helps him remain comfortable while communicating with you.

John Nolan Tips

I spoke to John Nolan, the author of *Confidential: Uncover Your Competitors' Top Business Secrets Legally and Quickly–and Protect Your Own*, now out of print. I've read everything that he's written for public consumption. Since John was so masterful in elicitation, I'm sharing some of his ideas here.

Nolan's Tip #1: Get the other person comfortable ASAP! Put your ego aside to help make the other person more comfortable throughout your conversation.

Nolan gauges the other person's motivation prior to selecting an elicitation technique. **Nolan's Tip #2:** If someone is boastful, John will push him into one-upmanship. John will say something about himself or his company, so that the other person says, "Well, let me tell you about mine." Similarly, if John offers a quid pro quo, he expects the braggart to offer something bigger or better.

I appreciate that John is a little playful in how he describes and uses elicitation techniques. This is one about betting when dealing with a person who is competitive.

John: "I bet you that no one at this trade show offers feature X." And the betting person is apt to come back with, "Oh yeah, well I do!" And proceeds to tell you all about it.

When John Nolan wrote his book, most conversations were conducted on the telephone although some were in-person.

Nolan's Tip #3: If on a phone call, one of the first things John did was to visualize the person. It made him feel more comfortable, which he sensed made the other person more comfortable. This is still a useful exercise as sometimes we use our mobile devices in audio mode. Other times you are transferred to a person you've never heard of, and don't know what she looks like. The transfer happens so quickly that you don't have time to look her up on the Internet or social media. Or you're using a video conferencing tool like Zoom and the other person doesn't show his face, and you were counting on that nonverbal communication. Or heaven forbid, the person is not on social media, so you don't know what he looks like and he doesn't do video chats.

Nolan's Tip #4: John is a big believer in monitoring the other person's breathing: its rate, depth and pace. You'll notice voice changes when a breathing pattern changes if you can't see who you are talking to. If you have a visual, it's much easier since shoulder position changes or hair movement—depending on length of hair—indicates a breathing pattern change. John taught me that mirroring a person's breathing improves rapport. I have noticed it's very effective and now it comes naturally to me.

> **Mirroring a person's breathing improves rapport.**

Nolan's Tip #5: John likes to observe when a person is not comfortable or cooperative during an in-person or virtual conversation. Some verbal and nonverbal behaviors include a nervous tick, fidgeting, cracking knuckles, going pale or red, tapping a foot, yawning, looking at his watch, changing posture or talking in a dull voice. Lower interest can be indicated by a hand pressing on the top back of the head.

John notes that after a while, elicitation can become second nature to you. Still, you can always improve.

Nolan's Tip #6: Learn observation skills. "If you are a big picture guy, you need to find a way to throttle it back and move mentally from the big picture down into the details or else the quality of the information you gather suffers dramatically."

chapter twenty-five

Elicitation Techniques: Case Studies

Some elicitation techniques complement each other
or can be used together.

Many who work in marketing, product marketing, competitive intelligence, sales and sales enablement use elicitation techniques. They may not realize they're using these techniques as they don't plan their conversations around elicitation techniques. Maybe they don't plan their conversations at all.

You're going to learn these techniques and how to use them consciously to become more effective at getting what you're looking for from the person to whom you're speaking. With practice, they will come naturally to you.

You'll relate with some elicitation techniques better than others. I recommend you start by using the ones that come naturally to you. There is one I really don't like, so I don't use it.

Some elicitation techniques complement each other or can be used together. The idea is not to repeatedly use the same elicitation techniques but to float from one to the other during a conversation. This is referred to as "stacking" in John Nolan's book, *Confidential*. I refer to it as combining elicitation techniques. I'll show you how this works in Chapter 29, *Combining Elicitation Techniques and Bonus Elicitation Techniques!*

There are some 40 elicitation techniques, and I describe 13 verbal elicitation techniques in detail and several others as a bonus in Chapters 26-29. Elicitation techniques can also be body language to encourage sharing. Seven of them were shared in Chapter 19, *Execute: Be Visually Friendly.* There are also shades of degree within the elicitation techniques that are discussed.

I will share some examples from my projects as I describe the elicitation techniques.

1. Operating Room (OR) Interim Nurses Research Project (cold calls)

2. Electrical Measurement Meters Project (cold calls)

3. Trade Show collection, a ripe area for using elicitation techniques (in-person)

4. Experience from calls with customers (scheduled calls)

1. Operating Room OR Interim Nurses Research Project
My client wanted me to study healthcare best practices among firms who hire interim operating room nurses. I had to call several companies to become enlightened. Before doing so, I studied their websites, read some articles about the interim nursing business and learned about the people who work in this field. I learned that there was a shortage of operating room (OR) nurses and that there was little training for OR nurses in nursing school. It was mostly learned on the job. All the companies in this business were small privately held companies, so I had to get it right when I called each company. No pressure, right?

The most interesting company was the market leader, which is the company I will focus on. They shared officer bios and videos on their website. One of the videos was the VP of Marketing. He was very formal, conservative, and seemed to be confident and arrogant by how he spoke and held himself.

After a close look at their website, I dialed the main number. As I couldn't share which geographic territory my customer was in, the receptionist transferred me to the VP of Marketing, much to my dismay. I had hoped to get connected to a salesperson who I knew would be forthcoming. I wondered if this marketing executive would tell me anything. Maybe he would, as he seemed to be egotistical and confident about himself. He had the bragging rights of working for the market leader and being the first company in this business.

When interviewing and using elicitation techniques on a cold call, which this was, you need to quickly figure out who you are talking to and how you think he will be motivated to share with you. In this case, not 10 minutes before the call I had reviewed the executives' videos, so thankfully this was fresh in my mind.

My client was interested to learn about the best practices for hiring OR nurses, specifically temporary full-time OR nurses. These nurses take assignments in hospitals around the United States, requiring them to set up temporary residences with every assignment. I found out these nurses would be on an assignment anywhere from three months to two years at a hospital before moving on to the next assignment.

The VP of Marketing was eventually forthcoming, but it was a challenge at the start of our conversation!

2. Electrical Measurement Meters Project

I mentioned this project earlier in this book, but not in much detail. I was studying handheld electrical measuring meters. I needed to talk with those who used these meters, mostly tradespeople, but also a few handymen and home repair guys. I wanted to learn how they used these instruments; how and why they had made their purchasing decision; what they thought about the performance of the meter they were using; how soon they would be replacing it or buying an additional meter; and whose meter they would likely purchase and why.

Before this project, I knew very little about electrical measurement meters, so I had to learn the industry before I called the tradesmen. Before making any calls, I learned how these instruments were used, and that durability and safety were very important. It takes some skill to use these instruments, and there is quite a variety of these meters in the marketplace. I went to some retail and wholesale stores so I could see and handle the instruments. I asked salespeople what they thought about the various manufacturers' instruments. They were surprised to see a woman with an interest in handheld meters that measured electrical properties. They happily engaged with me, once they realized that I might even know what I was talking about.

I searched YouTube and found experts who took the instruments apart to show the superiority of one manufacturer's meter over the others. I looked at Amazon reviews and read what people said about these instruments after purchasing them. I went to all the competitors' websites. Some of them had instrument tutorials and white papers that I read.

Armed with this information and with the intelligence my client shared, I got a good idea of the questions I should ask. With my client's assistance, I prepared an introduction as to what I was doing and why we needed the tradesperson's help without disclosing the client's identity. Then I re-ordered the questions the client wanted answered to discuss more general issues first about what they did for a living and how they used the instrument. These were not threatening topics. Then I worked my way to collect more detailed information like buying criteria, preferred brands and why. By the time we got to these, the tradespeople would be more comfortable talking to me. Lastly, I would ask about their age, since I figured by the end of the interview, we would almost be friends, and they wouldn't mind sharing.

My client gave me a list of customers, so I knew what company each person worked for and his job title (aside from the handymen). As these were mostly tradespeople, they were not active on social media, so I didn't waste my time searching there. If I didn't know the company's business, I looked it up before the call. That way I could warm up the call a bit with a comment or question about what it was like to work in his industry, for his company or in his position.

Even this small bit of personalization went a long way during these cold calls. They liked that I recognized and appreciated their profession. They felt like I was talking to them personally. If I made mistakes, which I did, they couldn't resist correcting me, especially as they noticed I had tried to understand their business before calling them.

I tried to put myself in their place. What might they be doing when I called them? I feared it would be tough to hear them since many worked in industrial spaces that are noisy. Would they hear their mobile telephone ring? How receptive would they be to my phone call interruption? Would they welcome a break?

Probably nobody called them to ask about their work and how they used these instruments. They might like to tell someone, since many worked by themselves doing installation, repair and maintenance work. However, it could work the other way. They might not be receptive to an interruption since they might be in the middle of a job. I needed to be sensitive to this and be flexible.

As all these tradespeople would be men, how would they react to a woman calling them with some knowledge about meters and their industry? Would they be intrigued by this or would they be put off since women don't work in this field? I hoped that they would like to talk with a woman who was interested in their work.

I had great success with this project once I got through to the person using the electrical measuring meter. Those I spoke to were cooperative. People seldom asked for their opinion or experience using these instruments. While they were pressed for time like anyone else, they wanted to be heard. I was happy to listen.

chapter twenty-six

Friendly Elicitation Techniques

You want to be more like Peter Falk
who played Lieutenant Columbo in a
long running American crime drama television series.

I'll start with the more friendly elicitation techniques that make you more appealing.

These include:

1. Expression of Mutual Interest

2. Flattery

3. Quid Pro Quo

4. Confidential Bait

5. Naivety

> **Naivety is a good elicitation technique since it often leads the other person to inform or correct you.**

Sharing a mutual interest, an experience you have in common, or flattery are good examples of friendly elicitation techniques. Quid pro quo or sharing a secret also engenders warm feelings. These techniques encourage the other person to trust you and feel good about conversing with you. Naivety is another good elicitation technique since it often leads the other person to inform or correct you.

1. Expression of Mutual Interest

Expressing a mutual interest often lowers the other person's defenses and opens conversation. Mutual interest can be a good icebreaker for your conversation but can also be used during other parts of the conversation.

Stay up on current events to see if you can find something you share in common. You can also listen for these during your conversation and spontaneously bring them up. I use this, especially at trade shows since you're in the same or a similar profession. That's a mutual interest and usually opens up a conversation!

Mutual Interest: OR Interim Nurses Project
Me: "You know, I really enjoy traveling too. I imagine that would also appeal to your workforce of interim nurses since they accept positions all over the US."

This was a great icebreaker, an effective way to start our conversation. That's often all I needed to say to get him talking about his business.

Mutual Interest: Electrical Measurement Meters Project
Me: "When you work with electricity, I bet safety is a key concern."

Tradesman: "Oh yes … in fact, we ended up buying this brand since one person's meter blew up in our factory."

He proceeded to tell me what he liked about this new brand, which was one of the brands my client wanted to learn about.

In customer interviews you can share a good value proposition, the mutual benefit for why you want to have this conversation.

I am usually following up from an email, so I reiterate it in so many words.

Examples of my followup emails:

"We want to continue to do the things you value, to discontinue what you don't and to develop products, services or features that will help grow your business."

"Thank you for agreeing to speak with me today. As mentioned, your feedback will help our company take the guesswork out of what needs improvement, what you'd like us to develop and what you value that we should continue to do."

"Thank you for your time today. In the interest of our ongoing business partnership, this conversation is part of our continuous improvement work. I'm sure your ideas and feedback will give us valuable input on how to better support you."

2. Flattery

Flattery often pulls a person into a conversation that otherwise would not take place. Everyone, whether prominent or very low on the totem pole, reacts positively to flattery.

Flattery will get you everywhere since it appeals to a person's ego. Often enough people get so little recognition that stroking their ego works.

Status elevation is best used on lower-level employees whether in the government or commercial sectors. When you offer praise for someone's work he tends to like you and is more willing to share information with you.

Make sure that the status elevation or recognition is authentic and deserved, not created. People can see right through this. Your insincerity will be noted for what it is, deception, and you won't be building up trust and she will dislike you. That is the opposite of good elicitation.

> **Flattery often pulls a person into a conversation that otherwise would not take place.**

More general examples include:

"I've heard you're the best ... an expert." Appeals to a person's expertise.

"You're the only one ...."

"I read your recent article in Forbes ...." (Special credit if you remember the date of the article.)

"Teach Me." You don't know much about a topic and ask the expert to elaborate on it.

Praise the person for a job well done!

Flattery: OR Interim Nurses Project

Executive: "So, why are you calling our company?"

Me: "I've heard you're the market leader in this industry, so I knew I had to call you."

He nodded his head in consent and we went from there.

Clearly, he was testing me to make sure I was sincere.

Flattery: Electrical Measurement Meters Project

Flattery was easy in the Electric Meter Instrument Project since I didn't use these instruments. But I did read up on them beforehand. I also saw and handled the products in stores.

Me: "I am calling you since you **use** these meters. There is no better source than you for what's good, bad or dangerous about these meters."

In another instance one tradesman told me he'd been an electrician for 33 years. I was very impressed with this and said, "I bet you've seen a lot of changes in this industry over that period of time." He told me how he had seen the industry change and where he thought the industry was going. Trends were a question my client had so this was valuable insight.

Flattery: Win/Loss Customer Interview

Me: "Thank you for taking the time to answer a few questions about the business decision you made to go with ACME a couple of months ago. I appreciate that you are willing to share your buying experience. There is no one better than our customers and prospects to give us ideas on how to improve our business practices and products."

Flattery: Trade Show

At trade shows flattery can be expressed for a new product, the best product, a company's reputation, a person's reputation, a professional looking booth, a great demo, etc.

Criticism

On the other hand, there is another side to flattery that is the opposite, criticism and deflation. Criticize an individual or organization in which the person has an interest in the hopes that the person will disclose information in defense.

Since humans need recognition, status deflation works particularly well with people who are egomaniacs. They will often provide additional information to prove you wrong. Criticism often works well with extroverts since they're verbal and more apt to defend the person or organization you're criticizing.

Deflating: "I hear that Competitor A has exceeded your share of market in Asia, particularly in China."

Colleague: "I don't know where you heard that, but that's not so. We are still the market leader in China since Competitor A's service is so bad there. We are losing share in Japan, but that's not such a big deal since the growth is really in China."

3. Quid Pro Quo

I'll share if you share. This is information you share that the other person values. This encourages people to match the information that you provide. It's simply human nature. Quid Pro Quo is a gesture of good faith and openness. You volunteer

Make sure that the information you provide is OK with your company to share.

information in the hopes of getting something in return. I often share a little tidbit about our company, and then she tells me a tidbit about her company in return and sometimes even more!

This beckons back to making sure that the information you provide is OK with your company to share. You also need to be prepared to answer some questions as this technique often brings them up. If you're not prepared, you may end up going down a rabbit hole from the unexpected questions the other person asks that you had not thought about and have no intention of answering.

Quid Pro Quo: Customer Calls
Customers are often curious to know what others have shared with me. They are also curious about the competition and what

your company has in the development pipeline. Many companies are cautious about sharing what's in their pipeline with good reason. Sometimes the product or service feature isn't available by their projected pipeline date, so they'd rather not share. On the other hand, if you get approval, you might share some of your pipeline to encourage the customer to tell you what the competitor has in theirs. Often enough your customer or prospect also shares their experiences about how the competitor sells against your company.

Quid Pro Quo: OR Interim Nurses Project

The man I interviewed in this OR Interim Nurses Project was an executive. He tested me like executives often do. I was so disappointed that I wasn't transferred to a salesperson since they are so much easier to talk with. Sales often doesn't seem to care that you are not likely to be their customer. They just talk.

This executive asked, "Who else are you talking to?" This was a surprise. I had to think quickly.

- Which competitors had I learned enough about to share at this point in my research?

- Which ones would he be most interested in hearing about, which in turn would encourage him to tell me more?

- Which competitors might I appreciate hearing supplemental information about since I heard conflicting information during previous interviews?

There were two competitors on my short list. I went with Competitor A, a low-price competitor who had a different pricing model from all the other competitors for their OR nurse interim services. I shared this with him, and discredited Competitor A's pricing model. This engaged him since he wanted to hear more about this competitor and why I didn't like their pricing model. From this point on he was quite chatty.

Quid Pro Quo: Electrical Measurement Meters Project
The tradespeople didn't care who else I was calling, but some wanted to know what I had learned about meter usage at other industrial companies. When I told them, they would share why and how they used the various meters at their shop. I think many of them were testing me since I was a woman working in a man's space. But they really opened up once I shared and realized I appreciated the risky environment they worked in.

Reflected Quid Pro Quo
Reflected Quid Pro Quo has the same goal as Quid Pro Quo, but you are not sharing about your company, but about a competitor. For example, at trade shows I often talk about a mutual competitor to learn more. It has a similar effect as Quid Pro Quo, in that he often tells me more about his company's product or service as compared to the competitor. It's often a bonus as I learn more about the mutual competitor as well as the target company.

4. Confidential Bait. (Just Between the Two of Us)
Share seemingly confidential information in hopes of receiving confidential information in return. Confidential Bait is Quid Pro Quo at a higher level since it's a secret between two people.

Confidential bait works so well at trade shows.

People just can't keep secrets! Here are some examples of phrases that often lead to Confidential Bait.

- I shouldn't be telling you this, but ….

- I might get into trouble telling you this, but ….

- Oh dear … I've told you too much ….

- Did you hear? Company A is coming out with a new drug that will be announced tomorrow.

I don't know how often people have said to me, "I have never told anyone this before, but …."

Confidential bait works so well at trade shows. I use it when I want to learn if a rumor is just a rumor or if it's something we should be concerned about.

- I hear that Competitor B is introducing this disruptive product, feature, etc.

- Between you and me, Competitor C just won that big piece of business.

Either of these two bulleted examples could be combined with an Erroneous Statement to see if he "corrects" you. (See in Chapter 27, *Elicitation Techniques: Erroneous Statements.*)

5. Naivety

Your naivety can lead a more knowledgeable person to instruct you. You can pretend to be ignorant about a topic to encourage him to educate you. I don't need to pretend as I am somewhat naïve. I don't know as much as the other person about what we're discussing. They're happy to educate me. This technique tends to work with both introverts and extroverts.

On the other hand, I've learned if you're looking to get information you don't want to come across as stupid, just less knowledgeable than the person you're talking to. I am interested in your discipline, your product or your market, but I am less educated about it. You want to be more like Peter Falk who played Lieutenant Columbo in a long running American crime drama television series. He used naivety continuously with suspected criminals.

The idea is to get the person talking. You're putting yourself in an inferior position to the person you're talking to ... purposefully.

A common phrase I use: "I was wondering if you might know about ...?" or simply, "I wonder about ...?"

Naivety: OR Interim Nurses Project

Me: "You know I have done a lot of work in hospital health care but I am not as familiar with OR nurses. I am not a registered nurse. I hope you can tell me a little more about how this business works."

Naivety: Electrical Measurement Meters Project

The tradesmen were not expecting a woman to be fluent in volts and amps. I declared I was not an electrician or an electrical engineer. But I appreciated what they did for a living and how careful they had to be when working with electricity. Since so few people asked about their work, the tradesmen were happy to share.

When one tradesman told me he used a competitor's meter, I told him I only knew how to operate the market leader's instruments, so I wondered how they might compare and why he chose the brand he selected. He went on for about 15 minutes and I hardly said a word.

chapter twenty-seven

Provocative Elicitation Techniques

Sometimes, you need to get people agitated
to get them to open up.

These elicitation techniques won't necessarily make you popular, but they often get the other person to open up. I tend to be somewhat playful with these. I don't threaten the other person with my tone of voice or with my body language on a video call or in an in-person meeting.

These include:

1. Provocative Statements

2. Opposing Stand

3. Unbelieving Attitude

4. Complaining

5. Erroneous Statements

6. Oblique References

Sometimes, you need to get people agitated to get them to open up. That's when you want to challenge them using such techniques as a provocative statement, taking an opposing stand, disbelief or even complaining.

1. Provocative Statements

The provocative statement is used to trigger a question in response, which usually sets up another elicitation technique such as quid pro quo, disbelief, naivety or criticism. It's disarming and deflecting and can be used any time during a conversation.

Provocative Statement: OR Interim Nurses Project
Me: "I understand that Competitor X offers mentoring services to their interim workers."

The executive retorted, "No Way. One of our interim workers left them since all the mentoring she got was a bottle of wine!"

It was unusual that he didn't ask me another question, but I think he wanted to make the point that the competitor didn't offer mentoring. I was happy to learn this since my client wanted to know if anyone offered mentoring services. These nurses worked long distances from home for several months at a time.

Provocative Statement: Electrical Measurement Meters Project
One of the tradesmen complained about the market leader's price and really couldn't say anything positive about the instrument.

Finally, I almost scowled at him, "You are using the product, yet you have nothing good to say about it!" Suddenly, he opened up and told me he liked the ergonomics of the market leader's instrument and that it was water resistant. It fit in his hand so nicely. All the competitors' electric meter instruments were bulky, like bricks. They were heavier and awkward to hold. Being water resistant was also important as he lived in the Seattle area where it is often rainy.

Provocative Statement: Customer Interview

Me: "You'd be surprised to know that we (Company B) are losing more deals to Competitor A than we used to."

Customer: "Really?"

Me: "Yah, their latest maintenance software upgrade is just killing us."

Customer: "Oh, that …. I could tell you about their maintenance software if you'd like …." And he continued to tell me.

A provocative statement can also be toned down by using a more passive approach.

For example, "I don't suppose that your family relocated to Germany too." Or, "I don't suppose that you know about …."

Challenging Statement

A challenging statement is a twist from a provocative statement. It's an intentional denial of credibility meant to provoke clarification along with more detailed information.

Me: "Wow, you said it only costs you $100 to manufacture each unit. That can't be right. The materials you use would leave you no profit."

Then he proceeded to tell me about component pricing, sourcing, etc.

2. Opposing Stand

Purposely take the opposite stand from what the other person just said.

In more general terms, here are some phrases to start a sentence with an opposing stand.

"You know, I don't think that's true."

"I can't imagine how you could do this, given what you just said."

"I don't agree with …."

Opposing Stand: OR Interim Nurses Project
Me: "I understand you'll only do interim placement but not permanent placement. As the market leader, I thought you'd be a one-stop shop for all OR nurse placements."

I knew they didn't do permanent placement. I got him a little angry, which got him talking to defend his company's position as the market leader. He shared more of the specifics of their interim placement, which is what I was looking for. Such as, "We don't do any consulting and focus strictly on interim placement."

Opposing Stand: Electrical Measurement Meters Project
I just couldn't get any valuable information from one of the tradesmen. He used the market leader's product but I couldn't understand why. He said the metering instruments were all similar to each other, and that the market leader's products were more expensive.

Me: "I don't understand why you use the most expensive equipment if you think all the instruments are comparable to each other." (Opposing Stand)

That's when he finally told me that the market leader's product was far more reliable than any of the competitors' products, and their performance was better too … and on and on ….

Opposing Stand: Customer Conversation
In my telco sales days, my competitors would only price out the cost of their telecommunications equipment in their proposals.

They did not include network fees, which were required to get dial tone. My price included the equipment cost plus the network fees! Opposing stand was a great technique to use when my customer told me that the competitor's price was much cheaper than my company's price.

> Customer: "Their price is 20% to 30% less than yours."
>
> Me: "You know that isn't true." (Opposing statement)
>
> Customer: "How can you say that?"
>
> Me: "They don't include network fees that you will have to pay for to make their equipment work." (Provocative statement)
>
> Customer: "Oh … do tell." Or "Oh, really? How much would network fees add to their cost?"

I would explain the total cost of the competitor's solution, which included network fees. Our company's price might still be a little higher, but adding network fees to a competitor's equipment price often leveled the playing field.

Other times customers didn't give me a chance to explain the full cost and bought the competitor's product. Sadly, they would find out later that the competitor's price only included the equipment cost. They would have to call the phone company to order network service to hook up the competitor's equipment at an additional cost.

3. Unbelieving Attitude

Disbelief – They feel like they must educate you to get you to believe.

Indicate disbelief or opposition to prompt a person to offer information in defense of his position. This technique gets the person to explain why you're wrong and why he is right. This is human nature. You get more information in a nonthreatening way. You can be playful with this technique.

Unbelieving Attitude: OR Interim Nurses Project

Me: "You've got to be kidding. I find it hard to believe you've been in Interim Management for 50 years!"

No other company had been in this market this long. The executive had proudly mentioned this in the video I had watched on its website just before making the call. I hoped this approach would work. It did. He had to tell me more about why his company was the market leader.

Unbelieving Attitude: Electrical Measurement Meters Project

Another easy one was when people would tell me their age at the end of the interview. They often sounded younger than their actual age.

Me: "Really! You sound a lot younger than that!"

After that, they often shared nuggets showing their experience and wisdom, just as we'd be hanging up. I wouldn't have gotten this information otherwise.

Unbelieving Attitude: Customer Calls

Me: "I can't believe you chose our solution after all the good things you said about Competitor A."

I have used this line in several Win/Loss conversations, and it gets a great response. The customer often gets defensive and tells you what they like about your company's solution. Sometimes people don't realize how much they have complained until you call them on it.

Unbelieving Attitude: Trade Shows
There are so many ways to use the Unbelieving Attitude at trade shows.

"I can't believe that Company X only has a small presence at this conference." (Find out why and what's behind that and often much more.)

"I can't believe how much Competitor X has grown in the last year."

"I was surprised to hear that Competitor X hired away (Joe Blow) from your company."

They just can't help but tell you more. What's great about trade shows is they're not recording your conversations, so the muddle in the middle is often forgotten by the end of the day if not sooner!

4. Complaining
Many people just love to complain. Some people complain more than others. You complain about an individual, an institution or industry expert. This often makes the other person more defensive, and he'll often tell you more to assuage your complaint. Often it will be an inadvertent disclosure in the name of defense.

I simply complain about something I want to know more about.

Complaining: Electrical Measurement Meters Project
Some tradesmen chose a less expensive meter instrument since the market leader's product was substantially more expensive. I figured that pricing would get them to complain, and I hoped they would share other reasons why they chose a less expensive alternative.

Me: "So it sounds like your major complaint with the market leader's product was price. How dare they charge so much more!"

Tradesman: "That's right. They are 30% higher than anyone else in the market."

Me: "So I'm thinking price was the biggest reason you chose Competitor X's product." (Presumptive Statement)

The answers varied considerably, but we got past pricing and found out other reasons why they bought a competitor's instrument.

Complaining: Customers

Customers complain about pricing more than anything else. Be prepared to deal with this. You might suggest that the competitor's price is lower since they have poor customer service. You've heard this from others you're speaking to. Maybe they don't agree with this. They are apt to give you more reasons why the competitor's price is lower. They will expect you to convince them that your product or service merits a higher price if that's the case.

Another great target to complain about is regulation and compliance with rules. The EPA, FDA and OSHA are some key US regulatory agencies. Find out which regulatory agency checks up on the industry you're working in.

5. Erroneous Statements

This elicitation technique sometimes requires a little acting but can be a lot of fun and is very useful. I know many people are not comfortable using this technique.

Deliberate false statements make a knowledgeable person want to correct you. You say something you know is wrong in the hopes that the person will correct your statement with the right information.

These days it's relatively easy to find something that can be misquoted, misunderstood or mistaken. It only needs to be a little off for the other person to correct you.

I do this sometimes to test my sources, when I suspect someone is not the expert I expected he'd be. If he doesn't correct me, then I figure he probably isn't a knowledgeable source. Bear in mind that most people can't help but correct me, especially as a woman with my personality.

Erroneous Statement: Electrical Measurement Meters Project
I would state that if they bought the market leader's instrument, it must be due to price. I knew that was not true since the market leader's instrument was the most expensive one. This was one way I found out if he was using the market leader's meter.

If he was using the market leader's instrument, he would immediately correct me and complain about its high price. Then he would let me know why he bought the market leader's product despite the higher price, which is what we were looking for. If he was using a competitor's instrument, he would also tell me why he bought it, which was usually because it was cheaper and good enough.

Erroneous Statement: Customers
During Win/Loss conversations, when I suspect the person I'm interviewing isn't the right person, I will provide some product information I know is wrong to see if he'll correct me. If he doesn't correct me, I realize I must find another person who understands the product. Most people are happy to refer me to the right person and are glad not to be put on the spot. Minus a referral, I go back to Sales to find the right customer contact.

Erroneous Statement: Trade Shows

I'll mention a rumor I've heard about the wrong competitor or product to see if he corrects me. I have learned more information this way, since people just want to be right and to inform me that I'm wrong. Usually, all I have to do is listen. It's amazing!

Erroneous Statement: How Many Salespeople Cover the Western United States?

Me: "It must be difficult to cover the Western states by yourself." (Erroneous statement: Since I knew he didn't.)

Salesperson: "Actually, I cover California, Washington and Arizona."

Me: "Wow, I can't believe that you cover those states all by yourself. California would be challenging enough!" (Unbelieving attitude)

Salesperson: I have two reps helping me and five reps cover the other Western states other than Alaska and Hawaii.

6. Oblique References

This is my least favorite elicitation technique since I tend to be a more direct person. The idea is to discuss one topic that may provide insight into a different topic. Comments are made indirectly, in either a positive or negative light, which generate either defense or criticism. It works on the subtle power of suggestion.

You make a comment about a related topic taking advantage of people's tendency to go from the general to the specific.

You refer to a topic that is related to what you're looking for. For example, you want to know if a competitor is going to downsize its finance department. Mention that your company's HR department is downsizing. This plants the seeds in the other person's mind about downsizing.

It's time to show you how multiple elicitation techniques can flow into a conversation.

Oblique References and Multiple Elicitation Techniques:
Find Out Where They're Losing Share in Beverages

Me: "How are things with your family these days? Have you been on any good trips lately?" (Small Talk)

Colleague: "We're getting along fine. We just got back from Amsterdam a week ago. Great place to visit."

Me: "You know my dad always liked Amsterdam. By the way, the other day our colleague Joe said that your company and several others were losing share in the food business to Tyson Foods. I don't know where he hears this stuff, but I disagreed with him since he often gets confused about these things." (Oblique Reference and Disbelief)

Colleague: "Well, actually, we haven't lost share in the food business, but sadly we're losing share in the diet beverage industry. Competitor X has introduced a new product that has just taken off."

Me: "Oh, I'm sorry to hear that. It sounds like you were surprised by this introduction." (Presumptive Statement)

Colleague: "I am embarrassed to admit it but we were. Food and beverage are so competitive. Our revenue from diet beverages went down 5% last quarter. We need to do some in-depth research to get to the bottom of this. I want to find out why customers are buying Competitor X's diet drink, and to determine if it's sustainable. You know how fickle the public can be. They jump on something and six months later, they go back to their old habits."

Me: "I sure do." (Nodding my head, agreeing)

Me: "It's more interesting to talk about travel, don't you think? We went to Singapore last month. Loved all the tropical flowers there. Have you been there?" (Small Talk)

Colleague: "Yes, I was there for a conference a couple of years ago. It was a long plane ride to get there, but a great conference, and we stayed there for a few extra days."

Me: "What did you think of Singapore?" (Small Talk)

Colleague: "Loved all the culture and the great business vibe. I'd like to go back sometime!"

Me: "Great! I'll look forward to hearing about your next trip!"

This short example shows how you start with some small talk questions that are relevant to the person you're talking to. Then you use elicitation techniques to get what you're looking for. I started with the oblique and the disbelief elicitation techniques in the same sentence. I quickly got my answer. Then I used a presumptive statement since it sounded like my friend's company was surprised by the competitor's market entry. They were and he gave me a percentage of revenue lost. Then I egged him on until I could get the conversation away from business and back to travel. The idea behind using elicitation techniques is that they'll remember the small talk questions and the end of your conversation more than your conversation using elicitation techniques, which is the information you seek. So presumably he would remember our discussion around travel more than the business conversation.

But remember, all bets are off about forgetting conversation using elicitation techniques if the conversation is recorded, which they are often enough these days. Companies can use AI to make sense of it, and the information can be easily retrieved and analyzed.

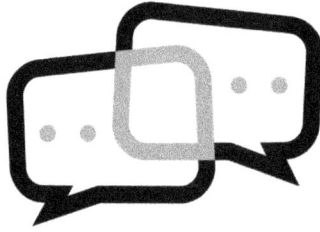

chapter twenty-eight

Two Important Elicitation Techniques

Resist the temptation to respond too quickly to the answer—
you'll discover something almost magical.

I saved my two favorite elicitation techniques for the last since I use them in almost every conversation.

1. Bracketing

2. Silence

I had mentioned both of these earlier, but I'd like to give you an example of how I've used them in elicitation.

1. Bracketing

I often use this technique towards the end of a conversation, when we've covered most of the information I'm looking for.

> **Bracketing is best used to learn specific quantitative information.**

Yet there are some details I still lack, or I need further quantitative detail than what the other person has shared.

You can use bracketing to get numbers like a guestimate. Let's do a sales example.

Me: "It must take between 300 and 400 salespeople to service California." (Presumptive Statement and Bracketing)

Salesperson: "Actually, it's more like 500."

Me: "Wow, that sounds like a lot!" (Disbelief)

Salesperson: "Well, only 50 of them are in field sales."

Me: "So, I assume most of your salespeople are telemarketers." (Presumptive statement shows I'm listening.)

Salesperson: "A few hundred work in telemarketing centers in San Francisco, Los Angeles, and San Diego. And about 50 work remotely on demand."

Bracketing is best used to learn specific quantitative information like pricing, revenue, annual growth, margin or salary. Offer a range that's fairly broad at the outset, but not too broad. Through successive conversation, narrow the range until you get close to the price or the percentage difference. Usually, I will suggest an upper and lower bracket that are realistic, so people take me more seriously. They'll presume that I know something about the business I'm asking about.

If you offer too wide a bracket, you risk losing your credibility. They might think you're fishing, trying to get at something that you know nothing about or that you're being too smooth, and they see right through you. Although you can purposefully make the bracket range wrong in an erroneous statement if your goal is to determine whether or not the person is a legitimate expert.

Bracketing: OR Interim Nurses Project

Me: "I understand that interim candidates work at each hospital from three months to one year."

Executive: "Yes, that's true. Our minimum contract is for three months with a 3-month extension. We find that the average interim OR nurse takes a 6-month contract. We're happy to extend it if the nurse gives us 30 days advance notice in writing."

I wanted to find out the length of the average contract, so was happy he shared this. We were pretty far into the conversation by the time I brought this up.

Bracketing: Win/Loss Interviews

I use bracketing most often in Win/Loss Interviews to get at price.

Me: "I heard from procurement that we were 20% to 30% higher."

Customer: "Closer to 20%."

Me: "Frankly, I thought it was 15% to 20% higher."

Customer: "I think that's right."

This approach usually works. Since I know what price my company offered, I can easily calculate the approximate amount the competitor charged.

Sadly, sometimes I learn that the sales team did such a bad job explaining the price, and that was a major reason they lost the sale! The customer was confused and didn't want to deal with it.

Sometimes people tell you exact figures. This is where ethics comes in with CI collection. What do you share with your management or your client if you're a consultant? I've detailed it in Chapter 7, *Plan: Prepare Your Introduction and Ethics.*

2. Silence

Many are uncomfortable with silence, especially extroverts. It's a gift that lets people collect their thoughts. If you have a chatty person, just remain quiet and let him talk.

Extroverts often fill the silence with words. Don't feel like you need to say much once they get going except to guide the conversation and end it on a more personal note that has nothing to do with business such as travel, movies, sports or current events.

> In any conversation, be respectful and give the other person time to collect her thoughts.

Silence: Electrical Measurement Meters Project
Most of the tradesmen I spoke to in Texas for this project were very friendly. They volunteered more information than anyone else. Many of them even thanked me at the end of the interview when I should have been thanking them.

Other times you need to shut a person down, so you must interrupt and mirror or paraphrase what he's just said and move onto the next point in your conversation. I find that if I use the complaining elicitation technique to make my next point, he'll move on and then I can be silent again since he's a talker.

In any conversation, be respectful and give the other person time to collect her thoughts. If you rush her, she will sense that and won't be as comfortable sharing.

Especially when you probe deeply, that's a great time to be silent.

Journalist Jim Lehrer described how to pause in a conversation.

"If you resist the temptation to respond too quickly to the answer, you'll discover something almost magical. The other person will either expand on what he's already said, or he'll go in a different direction. Either way, he's expanding his response, and you get a clear view into his head and heart."

Try counting to three or five if you can stand it—after the other person answers a tough or thoughtful question. This method can be agonizing at first, but when used with empathy, silence works wonders to develop a deeper rapport between two people.

Since our natural tendency is to fill in silence, the pause can also work as a power play in a tougher scenario like salary negotiation. American talk show host Dick Cavett explained how he employed a tough-love style when interviewing guests.

"You can hold someone with silence and make them go on. You tend to feel you need to fill all dead air. There are times when if you just say no more than 'uh-huh,' and pause, they'll add something out of a kind of desperation that turns out to be pretty good. Let them sweat a little and then they'll come up with something that they were perhaps not going to say."

chapter twenty-nine

Combining Elicitation Techniques and Bonus Elicitation Techniques!

Always quote reportable facts …
there is enough fake news out there
without me adding to it.

Now that I've described elicitation techniques individually, it's time to show how a conversation flows by combining multiple elicitation techniques. I have pulled this dialog from the OR Interim Nurses Research Project shared in Chapters 26, 27 and 28.

Combining Multiple Elicitation Techniques: OR Interim Nurses Research Project

Me: "You know I really enjoy traveling too. I guess that would also appeal to your workforce of interim nurses since they work all over the US." (Mutual Interest)
(Such an icebreaker would work with most people but not this executive.)

Executive: "So, why are you calling our company?"

Me: "I've heard you're the market leader in this industry, so I knew I had to call you." (Flattery)
I could feel him nodding his head in agreement.

Executive: "Well, we have been in the business for 50 years, much longer than anyone else, so we know what we're doing in this business."

Me: "You've got to be kidding. I find it hard to believe you've been in Interim Placement for 50 years!" (Disbelief)

Me: "No other company has been in the business longer than 20 years." (Flattery)

Executive: (Still testing me) "Who else are you talking to?"

Me: "The most interesting one was competitor A. They appear to offer a low price using a pricing methodology that is different from everyone else in the marketplace." (Quid Pro Quo)

Executive: "That's true, but I hear they are not good at recruiting quality interim nurses. You know, you get what you pay for. Also, I wonder if their pricing model is sustainable. They've only been in the business for two years."

Me: "Uh Huh." (Passive agreement, listening)

Me: "You know I have done a lot of work in hospital health care, but I am not as familiar with OR nurses. I am not a registered nurse. I am hoping you can tell me a little more about how this business works." (Naivety)

Executive: "It's a challenging business since there is a shortage of OR nurses. They're aging out. We attract the best quality nurses for our clients. We have an extensive system to check them out before we hire them. It's not everyone who can handle the stress of moving around the country to different cities and hospitals without getting burnt out."

Me: "I understand that Competitor B offers mentoring services to their interim workers." (Provocative Statement)

Executive: "No Way! One of our interim workers left them since all the mentoring she got was a bottle of wine!"

Me: "I understand you'll only do interim OR nurse placement but not permanent placement. As the market leader, I thought you'd be a one-stop shop for all placements." (Opposing Stand)

Executive: "Oh no, we'd never do permanent placement. We specialize and stay focused on interim OR nurse placement. There are so many logistical challenges with interim placement, and we have processes in place to deal with them effectively. We don't do any consulting and focus strictly on OR nurse interim placement."

Me: "You know, Competitor B told me that they do healthcare consulting, but I hear it's consulting light." (Provocative Statement)

Executive: "Oh yah, I'm here to tell you they just provide the interim worker, very little else. We have employees here who were dissatisfied both with this competitor's so-called mentoring support—which it really isn't—and their alleged consulting. They simply aren't in this space."

Me: "I understand that interim OR nurses work at each hospital from three months to one year." (Bracketing)

Executive: "Yes, that's true. Our minimum contract is for three months with a 3-month extension. We find that the average interim OR nurse takes a 6-month contract. We're happy to extend it if the nurse gives us 30 days advance notice in writing."

This was a challenging conversation since the executive was not Mr. Friendly and tested me several times before he started sharing. It wasn't until after the Quid Pro Quo that he opened up. I was lucky that I could guess his motivation (dominant, strong ego) from having watched his video on the company website.

Bonus Elicitation Techniques

I have just described 13 elicitation techniques in detail with examples. You can build off those detailed explanations with these eight that I feel need less description to understand and use.

Presumptive Statement: State a fact that can be either true or false. This builds on the human ego … the need to be right and to correct you. It works since the other person assumes you know what you're talking about. Sometimes you do and sometimes you don't, or you are guessing.

Quote Reported Facts: Reference real or false information so she believes that information is in the public domain. This is akin to a Presumptive Statement.

Partial Disagreement: For example, "Somehow, that isn't always the case." This is akin to a Provocative Statement.

Word Repetition: Listen generously. Repeat the right words to encourage more, but not all the words. Paraphrase or be playful.

Ask for a Favor: This appeals to people since it feels good to do a favor.

Deadline: You're under the gun and people can relate since who doesn't feel pressure under deadlines?

Time Constraint: Say you'll only take five minutes. This gets you in the door and makes people more comfortable talking with you since you're not going to take too much of their time. I have noticed people often become engaged in our conversation and will go on for 15 to 20 minutes.

Something of Interest: This is related to the Oblique Reference technique. Share what another company, another industry or another location has done in hopes that she'll share what her company is doing.

Presumptive Statement

I try to make presumptive statements that I believe are true. For example, in Win/Loss interviews, I'll often say, "I assume you were a key influencer." The person I am talking to usually is. But it's enough of a lead-in that he usually tells me how the buying decision was made and who participated in it without my need to ask.

Quote Reported Facts

I prefer to quote reported facts that are true to the best of my knowledge since I prefer not to reference false information. There is enough fake news out there without me adding to it.

chapter thirty

Elicitation Simplified

Part of listening is to observe changes
in how they look, act, speak and breathe.

I've shared my process chart Interview-Conversation-Elicitation
in Chapter 23 and John Nolan's Conversational Hourglass in
Chapter 24. Here is a simplified elicitation process chart, which
might be easier to follow now that we've gone through the details
of using elicitation techniques.

Elicitation Simplified

1. Outcomes Objectives	2. Personal History How to Converse
3. Successful Techniques	4. Watch for Changes

1. What are your objectives for this conversation? How do
   you want it to end?

2. What's your history/relationship with this person?
   Based on that, how do you connect? (school, military
   background, sports, hobbies, or a referral)

3. Which techniques have worked in the past with this type of person? (or this person if you know him) Of those, which are you most comfortable using?

4. As you converse, part of listening is to observe changes in how they look, act, speak and breathe.

As shown in the detailed write-up of elicitation techniques, you can combine them and also use them in digital communication. Let's say you're emailing an industry analyst who publishes newsletters on the topic you're researching, but you're not having any luck finding articles about a new feature or a new product.

You might approach the industry analyst with, "I have read your work in this area, but I haven't seen anything about this state-of-the-art product. I guess you don't think it's newsworthy." Flattery to acknowledge the industry expert and a little provocative to pique his interest.

chapter thirty-one

My Final Thoughts

What you learn during a conversation
is deep compared to any other form of communication.

So What? Now What?

My CI colleagues and elicitation students often ask how I conduct myself in conversation. Do I ask questions, or do I strictly use elicitation techniques? My students often grow weary when learning and using elicitation techniques in our role plays. Using elicitation techniques is a challenge like anything you learn for the first time. It took me years of practice. And I feel I can still improve!

You need to figure out what approach will make the person you're talking with comfortable for the conversation at hand. Each person you talk to is unique and your goals for every conversation vary, as they do for the person you're talking with.

There is not a one-size-fits-all approach to conversation.

In general, I like to use a blend of questions and elicitation. I find most conversations go best when I ask a few open-ended questions and then use elicitation techniques to keep the conversation flowing. Put another way, most people I speak with expect me to ask questions, but most of the time we're having a conversation.

Sometimes, you want the other person to remember your questions. When I conduct Win/Loss interviews, I am another marketing touchpoint for my clients and people expect questions. The questions I start with are usually about what he does for the company and how well he likes it if I sense he does. He might share the challenges he faces at work. I want him to remember the questions that show I care.

Then I get to the business of the call. In a Win/Loss conversation, I'll explain that this is his opportunity to let me know what his buying experience was like with the company's sales team that hired me. This is an open-ended approach that puts him in the driver's seat and almost always gets him talking about what is important.

But if you got nothing else from this book, I'm sure you realize that there is not a one-size-fits-all approach to conversation. Sometimes I change my approach on the fly depending on how the other person says, "hello." I realize my assumptions about how he would be are wrong. This can happen any time during our conversation. I have learned to observe this and to be ready to adapt.

You are ready to Loosen Their Lips!

I have decades of working with CI. With each new project, I always start with a Plan … something that I encourage you to do. Let's review what's important to think about or do to Loosen Their Lips!

Plan

Establish your goals for the conversation from the start to the end.

- What questions do you need to have answered?

- Do you need to talk with a person for answers?

- Why will someone want to answer your questions?

- Who is likely to have those answers? Several people?

- How might they answer each question? Build a decision tree for how you might respond or probe further.

- What can you find out in the digital space or from another person beforehand to warm up the conversation?

- How will you introduce yourself to this person?

- What are you planning or willing to share during the conversation?

- Are there ethical issues you need to consider? If yes, identify them and get answers.

Pre-Execution

Consider the 5Ps, her preferred communication style, and her sharing disposition.

What does that mean for how you'll communicate with her?

- How will you get grounded before this conversation?

- What is your broad intention for this conversation beyond what you're hoping to find out?

- How do you tend to come across during a conversation?

- What do think her motivation will be to share?

Execution

How will you connect with him for this conversation? Will someone else make the introduction?

- Meet the person virtually. Build rapport quickly. Be polite.

- Observe him visually and listen to his words (accent, speed, tone, breathing). Do they match his visual expressions?

- Observe his preferred communication style and sharing disposition. Match his communication style and expressions.

- Be flexible. Gauge the conversation. Observe changes in expression, tone and breathing.

- Listen closely. Acknowledge him and give him your undivided attention. Listen for what he doesn't say.

- Lay aside your preconceived notions. Your assumptions might be wrong.

- Question, converse, comment and probe appropriately.

- Use elicitation techniques throughout if they flow well with the person you're talking with.

- Keep your intuitive radar sharp. Some people misinform and are deceptive. Some are nervous or stressed.

- End your conversation on a positive note. Give the person a chance to add what you didn't think to ask. *Thank you* goes a long way and keeps the door open.

Analyze

- What was relevant from this conversation to meet your goals?

- Do you feel you received accurate information and truthful feedback?

- Do you have gaps yet to fill? Review the Collection Continuum. Where do you go next?

- How effective were you during this conversation? Were you ethical?
- What did you learn? What would you do differently next time if anything?

Just Do It!

You have learned how to engage with another person during a conversation. If you are thorough in preparation, you will be more relaxed and can listen fully since you are grounded. You won't be panicking about what you should ask next. You can also think of other angles and questions right on the spot that you hadn't considered since his comments may trigger them or cause you to doubt something you thought you had already correctly collected that his answer contradicts.

Go practice! You will have confidence, intelligence and intuition to be flexible enough for however the conversation flows. You know, conversations often don't go as planned. You will be ready for those left turns and have the judgment to either bring the conversation back or have a sense that the left turn will take you to more sharing and better information. You are equipped with the tools to prepare yourself to be thoughtful and flexible and to deal with the spontaneity of conversation without fear!

What you learn during a conversation is deep compared to any other form of communication. You listen to a warm voice. You observe facial expressions and other body movements. Conversation opens you up to a deeper relationship with the other person as compared to snippets, likes and other reactions from social media. You're vulnerable during a conversation and that's OK. That's humanity. Just do it.

Other forms of communication remain essential, and there will be more ways to communicate with the development of AI in its many forms … and whatever comes next. You need to use them too.

But don't neglect your conversation. The information I gathered in the stories I shared throughout this book would not have been possible without conversation, often multiple conversations. The information I gathered was not contained on the Internet, social media or the Cloud—only in people's brains. At the conclusion of these conversations, I had developed a relationship. I could reach out to the person again for another conversation, and the feeling was mutual.

That's the beauty and productivity of conversation. You learn a LOT from what the other person shares. It's a real time dialog. You gain information, ideas, other resources, and insight and you share too. You close sales! That's the power of conversation!

**Take the attitude of a student,
never be too big to ask questions,
never know too much
to learn something new.**
—**Og Mandino,** American author

In closing:
> Plan.
> Research.
> Get grounded.
> Connect.
> Listen.
> Observe.
> Probe.
> Be flexible.
> Stay curious.
> *You will Loosen their Lips!*

Endnotes

Chapter 1

Zena Applebaum, The 'Non' Among Us, p. 21. *A Practical Guide to Competitive Intelligence*. 2022. Edited by Zena Applebaum, Philip Britton, Alysse Nockels. Special Libraries Association.

Victoria Richard Hanna, Gathering Human-Centered Insights, p. 168. *A Practical Guide to Competitive Intelligence*. 2022. Edited by Zena Applebaum, Philip Britton, Alysse Nockels. Special Libraries Association.

Chapter 2

John Nolan. "Elicitation" by Kirk Richardson. *Competitive Intelligence Magazine:* Vol 17, Number 4, Oct/Dec 2014.

Empathy: Dr Brené Brown, *Atlas of the Heart: Mapping Meaningful Connection and the Language of Human Experience*. p. 120. 2021. Random House.

Empathy other focused: Ronda Dearing. Dr Brené Brown, *Atlas of the Heart: Mapping Meaningful Connection and the Language of Human Experience*. p. 142. 2021. Random House.

Kent Potter on interviewing. *Gaining Market Insight from Events* by Jonathan Calof, p. 40. 2021. Strategic and Competitive Intelligence Professionals.

Chapter 5

Generative AI: *The Wall Street Journal*, "AI in Process Automation." November 13, 2023.

Chapter 8

Mindfulness: Dr. Jon Kabat-Zinn. Mindful Jon Kabat-Zinn: Defining Mindfulness. Jan 11, 2017. *https://www.mindful.org/ jon-kabat-zinn-defining-mindfulness/*

Chapter 9

Judith Glaser passed away in 2018. Her book *Conversational Intelligence: How Great Leaders Build Trust and Get Extraordinary Results* is still available as of this printing.

Opening up: Rollin McCraty and Doc Childre, "Coherence: Bridging Personal, Social, and Global Health," *Alternative Therapies 6*, no. 4 (2010).

Chapter 12

Terry Gross quote. "6 Powerful Communication Tips from Some of the World's Best Interviewers," *Fast Company* by Courtney Seiter, Feb 11, 2014.

Chapter 15

JP Ratajczak Facial Expressions: *Gaining Market Insight from Events* by Jonathan Calof, p. 73. 2021. Strategic and Competitive Intelligence Professionals.

JP Ratajczak Visual Expressions: *Gaining Market Insight from Events* by Jonathan Calof, p. 73. 2021. Strategic and Competitive Intelligence Professionals.

Bob Berkman (Information Professional, Editor and Media Studies Professor) Defines Intuition. Source: Presentation – Intuition: Business Research in the Age of Truthiness, Cynthia Lesky. Special Library's Association – Competitive Intelligence Division, 2013.

Language Matters: Dr. Brené Brown, *Atlas of the Heart: Mapping Meaningful Connection and the Language of Human Experience*. p. 236. 2021. Random House.

Chapter 18

Louder Than Words by Joe Navarro and Toni Sciarra Poynter. p. 211. 2010. HarperCollins.

Joe Navarro. "Elicitation" by Kirk Richardson. *Competitive Intelligence Magazine*: Vol 17, Number 4, Oct/Dec 2014.

Chapter 21

Seena Sharp. "Elicitation" by Kirk Richardson. *Competitive Intelligence Magazine*: Vol 17, Number 4, Oct/Dec 2014.

Chapter 22

J. C. Carleson. "Elicitation" by Kirk Richardson. *Competitive Intelligence Magazine*: Vol 17, Number 4, Oct/Dec 2014.

Chapter 24

Katie Couric. "6 Powerful Communication Tips from Some of the World's Best Interviewers," *Fast Company* by Courtney Seiter, Feb 11, 2014.

John Nolan. "Elicitation" by Kirk Richardson. *Competitive Intelligence Magazine*: Vol 17, Number 4, Oct/Dec 2014.

Chapter 28

Journalist Jim Lehrer. "Taking a Page from the Great Interviewers" by Susie Adams. InteractStudio.com. *https://interactstudio.com/taking-a-page-from-the-great-interviewers/*

"The Art of the Interview: Dick Cavett on How to Elevate a Q&A" by Joe Berkowitz. *Fast Company*. Dec 4, 2012.

Ellen Naylor
CEO of Business Intelligence Source

Ellen Naylor is one of America's pioneers in competitive intelligence and Win/Loss analysis with over 40 years of experience across many industries. Ellen initiated Bell Atlantic's (Verizon's) competitive intelligence (CI) program for enterprise marketing in 1985.

Ellen founded Business Intelligence Source, a CI consultancy in 1993. She consistently helps clients beat the competition and make smarter tactical and strategic decisions.

Clients tell Ellen that conversation is her superpower. She enjoys listening to people's stories which they readily share with her. She skillfully engages people during video chats, phone and in-person conversations. Ellen has always been successful at uncovering hard to find information that provides insight for her clients.

Ellen shows you how to get people to open up to you and share valuable information in *Loosen Their Lips*. If you want to find out why you're winning and losing business—and retain more, check out her award-winning book, *Win/Loss Analysis: How to Capture and Keep the Business You Want.*

Ellen has delivered hundreds of competitive intelligence presentations, workshops and webinars for clients as well as at conferences and universities globally. Her most popular subjects are Elicitation and Win/Loss Analysis.

Ellen has contributed to the Strategic Consortium of Intelligence Professionals (SCIP), as a board member, author and frequent speaker. SCIP recognized Ellen with the Fellow and Catalyst awards in appreciation of her leadership and contributions to competitive intelligence. As a CI Fellow, Ellen contributes to the Council of Competitive Intelligence Fellows where she served as a board member at its inception.

Earning her BA in international studies from the University of Notre Dame, in the second class of graduating women, and her MBA at the Darden Graduate School of Business, Ellen understands business. She is fluent in French. Born and raised in Japan, Ellen weaves in international experience and culture with her consulting clients. She lives in Denver, Colorado with Rodgers, her artistic husband and their cats.

How to Work with Ellen Naylor

Ellen is an expert in Competitive Intelligence (CI), Elicitation, and Win/Loss Analysis.

With her 40+ years in the field, Ellen's skills are best used as a **Consultant, Instructor, Speaker** or **Mentor/Coach.**

As a Consultant, companies hire Ellen to help develop, improve or resuscitate their competitive intelligence programs. She is an expert at helping companies with opportunity analysis, i.e. finding the next good product or service to bring to the market! She enjoys developing Win/Loss programs for companies across many industries.

As an Instructor, Ellen offers customized training for Elicitation and Win/Loss Analysis. During Elicitation training you will learn how to capture the information you seek during a business conversation. It's not just for CI professionals, researchers and product marketers. Salespeople value Elicitation training since it helps them speed up their journey through the sales funnel; close more business; and quickly eliminate poor prospects.

Ellen's goal in **Win/Loss Instruction** is to provide you with her unique12-step Win/Loss process that will help you establish a world class Win/Loss program. You learn why you're winning and losing sales—directly from your customers and prospects.

Ellen is in hot demand as a **Speaker** in Elicitation and Win/Loss Analysis.

With her extensive experience, Ellen is paying it back by **Coaching** and **Mentoring** those who are students; just getting started in competitive intelligence; or entering the profession from another discipline such as sales, marketing or the intelligence world.

Contact Ellen Naylor

MOBILE +1 720-480-9499

EMAIL Ellen@EllenNaylor.com

WEBSITE www.EllenNaylor.com

LINKEDIN EllenNaylorColorado

In Gratitude

I started to write this book in 2018, so I have many people to thank!

Thank you to Judith Briles, CEO of The Book Shepherd who was my book mentor and editor. She helped me every step along the way from the initial manuscript to marketing … and kept me on track! She and Rebecca Finkel, our graphics artist extraordinaire, make a terrific book support team! Thank you to Rebecca, for the book cover design and the book interior.

Thank you to my dear husband, Rodgers Naylor, who helped me edit the book in so many ways, right up to the end. He also gave me ideas for formatting and explaining things more clearly. And we're still happily married!

I got the idea to write about elicitation and conversation from John Nolan, author of *Confidential: Uncover Your Competitors' Top Business Secrets Legally and Quickly – and Protect Your Own.* He was the first one to introduce me to elicitation techniques through his presentations and workshops in the 1990s. I listened! Thank you to John for all your support and creativity!

Thank you to my talented competitive intelligence colleagues who shared your stories for this book: Adrian Alvarez, Andrew Beurschgens, Amir Fleischman, Suki Fuller and John Thomson.

Thank you to those who shared their knowledge which contributed to this book: Zena Applebaum, Jonathan Calof, Victoria Richard Hanna, Kent Potter, Melanie Prudom, JP Ratajczak and Seena Sharp.

A BIG thank you to those who reviewed the book and/or endorsed it. Thank you to Babette Bensoussan, Andrew Beurschgens, Craig Fleisher, Jay Nakagawa and Laurie Young. I really appreciate your advice and support.

Thank you to those who gave me moral support along the way. Fouad Benyoub, Tracy Berry, Phil Britton, Scott Brown, Rich Caldwell, Claudia Clayton, Cynthia Cheng Correia, Kathleen Dean, Jonathan Dunnett, Parmelee Eastman, Ashley Eisinger, Barbara Fullerton, Zaven Gabriel, Chrissy Geluk, August Jackson, Arik Johnson, Derek Johnson, Karen Johnson, Cliff Kalb, Luis Madureira, Craig McHenry, Jim Miller, Andreas Mueller, Alysse Nockels, Alfredo Passos, Tim Powell, Ben Scheerer, Christopher Shrope, Melanie Siewert, Lindy Smart, Ryan Sorley, Vera Lúcia Vieira, Ana Valéria Medeiros Wanderley, Michelle Winter and Lori Wolfe. I hope I remembered everyone, and if I forgot you I apologize!

The following are additional resources that influenced my thinking.

1. Grounding

Amy Cuddy's Power Pose; Dr Andrew Weil's 4-7-8 Breathing; Dr. Andrew Huberman's education around breathing, especially how to benefit from breathing exercises; and meditation from Plum Village founded by Zen Monastic, Thích Nhất Hạnh.

2. Authors

Dr. Brené Brown: *Atlas of the Heart: Mapping Meaningful Connection and the Language of Human Experience*

Dr. Paul Ekman: *Emotions Revealed: Recognizing Faces and Feelings to Improve Communication and Emotional Life*

Judith Glaser: *Conversational Intelligence: How Great Leaders Build Trust and Get Great Results*

Daniel Goleman: *Emotional Intelligence: Why It Can Matter More Than IQ*

Raymond L. Gorden: *Basic Interviewing Skills*

Joe Navarro and Marvin Karlins, PhD: *What Every BODY Is Saying: An Ex-FBI Agent's Guide to Speed Reading People*

Risa Sacks: *Super Searchers Go to The Source: The Interviewing and Hands-On Information Strategies of Top Primary Researchers— Online, on the Phone, and In Person*

Sherry Turkle: *Reclaiming Conversation: The Power of Talk in a Digital Age*

Finally, I'd like to remember John McGonagle and his beloved wife, Carolyn Vella. They co-authored at least a dozen competitive intelligence books. John has written more book reviews than anyone I know. Not this time. He and his beloved Carolyn have passed. Their legacy lives on in the Carolyn Vella and John McGonagle Library at Mercyhurst University in Erie, Pennsylvania.

If you don't ask your customers and those who chose a competitor, you won't truly discover why you're winning and losing deals. Find out why buyers choose to do business with you or your competition. Learn how they went about making their buying decision.

If your company is struggling, losing its visibility or failing in growth projections, you need **Win/Loss Analysis.** Woven throughout are steps to gather and implement competitive intelligence, customer insight and strategic panache. You will pull insight to develop specific buyer personas.

With the guidance of **Win/Loss Analysis,** you will discover how to remove the guess work, and gain more business by conducting Win/Loss interviews with your customers and former prospects—after the buying decision has been made.

For over two decades, Win/Loss expert Ellen Naylor has guided executives and managers to world-class results with her 12-Step Win/Loss process. Now you will get her inside tips and secrets to lead your company to do the same.

Not convinced yet? Research shows that taking action from a formal Win/Loss program can improve win rates between 15 to 30 percent.

Win Loss
ANALYSIS

How to Capture and Keep the Business You Want

Ellen Naylor

www.ingramcontent.com/pod-product-compliance
Lightning Source LLC
Chambersburg PA
CBHW051256020426
42333CB00026B/3234